LORD LAWRENCE

D1859633

LORD LAWRENCE

SIR RICHARD TEMPLE

GYAN

Published by

GYAN

Gyan Publishing House
5, Ansari Road
Daryaganj, New Delhi-110002
Phone: 011-47034999, 9811692060
E-mail: books@gyanbooks.com

Distribution Network
gyanbooks.com
India, USA, Canada, UK, Australia, France

© Publisher

All rights reserved. No part of this work may be reproduced, stored, adapted, or transmitted in any form or by any means, electronic, mechanical, photocopying, micro-filming, recording or otherwise, or translated in any language, without the prior written permission of the copyright owner and the publisher.

ISBN: 978-81-212-8852-1 (PB)
First Published, 1889

2nd Impression 2023

Printed at: Gyan Press, Delhi.

The book is sold subject to the condition that it shall not, by way of trade or otherwise, be lent, resold, hired out, or otherwise circulated without the prior publisher's written consent.

LORD LAWRENCE
AUTHOR: RICHARD TEMPLE

English Men of Action

LORD LAWRENCE

LORD LAWRENCE

Engraved by O. LACOUR after a Photograph by MAULL AND POLYBANK

LORD LAWRENCE

BY

SIR RICHARD TEMPLE

London
MACMILLAN AND CO.
AND NEW YORK
1889

The right of translation and reproduction is reserved

CONTENTS

CHAPTER VII

CHAPTER VIII

CHAPTER IX

CHAPTER X

CHAPTER I

INTRODUCTION

JOHN LAIRD MAIR LAWRENCE was born in 1811 and died in 1879, being sixty-eight years of age. Within that time he entered the Civil Service of the East India Company, governed the Punjab then the most difficult province in India, took a very prominent part in the War of the Mutinies, was by many called the saviour of the Indian empire, and became Viceroy of India. By reason of his conduct in these capacities he is regarded as a man of heroic simplicity, and as one of the best British type, to be reckoned among our national worthies.

I shall write the following account of him as a man of action, partly from authentic records, but chiefly from personal knowledge. I was his Secretary during some of the most busy and important years when he was governing the Punjab, and one of his Councillors when he was Viceroy. My acquaintance with him began in 1851, and continued on intimate terms till 1870, from which time until his death I was separated from him by distance. Thus I have been in great part an eye-witness of what is to be related of him. My knowledge, too, of his views is derived, not from correspondence nor from private letters, but from verbal communication. For several years it was my chief duty so to imbue my mind with his policy and opinions that I might be able to express them in writing at a moment's notice.

He was a man of action as distinguished from a man of letters. He did not write a book nor contribute to periodical literature. Among his predecessors and successors in high office amidst the imperial affairs of India, some have been men either of letters or of literary culture; as for instance, Warren Hastings, Wellesley, Teignmouth, Mountstuart Elphinstone, Lytton. Though neither unlettered nor uncultured, he had no literary training nor did he possess that which would nowadays be called culture. Again, some of his predecessors and successors had acquired a considerable position either in political and parliamentary life at home or in imperial affairs abroad, as for example Amherst, Ellenborough, Hardinge, Dalhousie, Canning, Elgin, Mayo, Northbrook. But he derived his position solely from experience of India, knowledge of her people, and services rendered within her limits. The son of a poor and hardy veteran officer, he was essentially a self-made and a self-taught man. It is therefore interesting to learn how he came to make and teach himself thus grandly, and what was the process of the making and the teaching. For he had no wondrous gifts of intellect or imagination and few external graces. He never enjoyed the advantages of high education, of family connection, of contact with political life, of guidance from the lights of the age. He had to raise himself by his own up-heaving force, and to propel himself by his own motive power. Before him many great men have been singled out for greatness by every observer from their youth onwards. But he as a young man was never deemed remarkable, and almost up to his middle life he was not expected by his best friends to acquire greatness. Then the hour of difficulty came, and was followed by other hours harder and harder still; and he was found more and more to be the man for them all. From a good magistrate of a comparatively old district he became the administrator of a newly-annexed territory. Thence he rose to be Resident at a Native Court in time of trouble, and virtual governor of an arduous province. While thus occupied he was overtaken by the desperate tempest of the Mutinies, and he rode on the crest of every wave. Thence he was promoted in natural order to the supreme command in India. Thus he rose not by assumed antecedents nor by collateral advantages, but by proved merit in action. Doing lesser things very well he was tried in greater things, and he did them with equal efficiency. Tested in the furnace of fiery danger he showed the purest metal. Lastly, when elevated to the highest office he was still successful.

All this while, his qualities were for the most part those which are commonly possessed by British people. He evinced only two qualities in an uncommon degree, namely energy and resolution. But if he was not a man of genius in the ordinary acceptation of the term, there must have been a certain genius in him, and that was virtue. Such genius is indeed heaven-born, and this was the moral force which combined all his faculties into a harmonious whole and made him a potent instrument for good, a man of peace or of war, according to the requirements of right and justice. His virtue was private as well as political, domestic as well as public. He was a dutiful son, a faithful husband, a kind father, an affectionate brother, a steadfast friend. There have been men eminent in national affairs over whose life a veil must partially be thrown; but his conduct was unassailable even by those who assailed his policy and proceedings. However fiercely the light might beat on him, he was seen to be unspotted from the world. Again there have been statesmen who, vigilant as regards the public interests, have yet neglected their own concerns; but he was a good steward in small things as well as in great. He always found the means of meeting charitable demands; he was ever ready with trusty counsel for his friends; he managed a fund formed by himself and his brothers as a provision for their widowed mother. But, while upright and undaunted before men, he was inwardly downcast and humble before the all-seeing Judge. He relied on divine mercy alone, according to the Christian dispensation. Apart from the effect of his constant example in Christian action, he made no display of religion beyond that which occasion might require. In this cardinal respect as in all lesser respects he was unostentatious, excelling more in practice than in precept. Amidst the excitement of success in emergent affairs, he would reflect on the coming time of quiet and retirement. In the heyday of strength and influence he would anticipate the hour when the silver cord must be loosed and the golden bowl broken; when surrounded with pomp and circumstance, he would reckon up the moments when the splendid harness must be cast aside. In a word, massive vigour, simplicity and single-mindedness were the keynotes of his character.

In the following pages, then, the development of this character will be traced through many striking circumstances in distant fields of action, through several grave contingencies and some tremendous events. The portrait will, indeed, be drawn by the hand of affection. Nevertheless every endeavour will be made to preserve accurately the majestic features, to pourtray the weather-beaten aspect, to depict the honourable scars, the wrinkles of thought, the furrows of anxiety. In a word he is to be delineated as he actually was in gentleness or ruggedness, in repose or activity, in sickness or health.

His course, from the beginning to the end of life, should have a spirit-stirring effect on the middle class from which he sprung. For to his career may be applied the Napoleonic theory of a marshal's baton being carried by conscripts in their knapsacks during a campaign. With virtue, energy and resolution like his, British youths of scanty means, winning their places by competition, may carry with them to the Eastern empire the possibilities of national usefulness and the resources for conquering fortune in her noblest sphere.

Moreover, a special lesson may be learnt from him, namely that of endurance; for he was, in the midst of energetic life, often troubled and sometimes even afflicted by sickness. In early life he seemed to have been born with powerful robustness; but as a young man he suffered several times from critical illness, and in middle age ailments, affecting chiefly the head, grew upon him like gathering clouds. As an elderly man he was prematurely borne down to the dust of death, while according to ordinary hope he might yet have been spared for some years to his family his friends and his country. If anything could add to the estimation in which he is held, it is the remembrance that when he magnificently swayed the Punjab his health was fitfully uncertain, that it was still worse when he stemmed the tide of the Mutiny and Rebellion, that it had never been really restored even when he became Viceroy, and that during the performance of deeds, always arduous and often heroic, he had to struggle with physical pain and depression as well as wrestle with public emergencies.

But though he might have added something to the long list of his achievements had his life been prolonged, still the main objects of his existence had been fulfilled, and he died neither too early nor too late for his fame. Even if it cannot be said of him that he lived long enough to be gathered to his fathers like a full shock of corn, still there is a fulness and a completeness in his career. To his memory may be applied the lines of Schiller on a dead hero: "He is the happy one. He has finished. For him is no more future here below. For him destiny weaves no webs of envy now. His life seems spotless, and spreads out with brightness. In it no dark blemish remains behind. No sorrow-laden hour knocks to rouse him. He is far-off beyond hope and fear. He depends no longer on the delusive wavering planets. For him 'tis well for ever. But for us, who knows what the dark-veiled hour may next bring forth!"

CHAPTER II

EARLY LIFE

1811-1829

HE who would understand this story aright must stretch the wings of his imagination for a flight across the ocean to the sunny shores beyond. In these northern latitudes sunshine is regarded as genial and benignant, but in those regions the sun is spoken of by the natives as cruel and relentless. It is with fierce rays that he strikes the stately architecture, the crowded marts, the dusty highways, the arid plains, the many-coloured costumes, the gorgeous pageantry,—in the midst of which our action is laid, and which in their combination form the theatre where the mighty actors of our drama are to play their parts. But not in such a climate nor amidst such scenes were these actors born and bred. In the time of youth,—when the physical frame is developed, and the foundation of the character is laid,—their stamina were hardened, their faculties nursed, their courage fostered, under the grey skies and misty atmosphere, in the dales and hills, amidst the green fields and the smoky cities of Great Britain and Ireland.

The village of Richmond is situated in the North

Riding of Yorkshire at the western base of the hills which flank the Westmoreland plateau, and near the head-waters of the Swale, an affluent of the Ouse. In the year 1811 it formed the headquarters of the Nineteenth Regiment of Foot, of which Alexander Lawrence was the Major.

Here John Lawrence was born on March 4th, 1811: being the eighth in a family of twelve children. His sister Letitia, his elder brothers George and Henry, his younger brother Richard, will be mentioned in the following narrative. His brother Henry, indeed, was closely associated with some of the events to be related hereafter.

The parents were people of British race domiciled for some generations in Ulster. The mother was a descendant of John Knox the Scotch reformer, and the daughter of a clergyman in the Church of England, holding a cure in Donegal. The father had run a military career for full fifteen years in India and Ceylon, and had been among the leaders of the forlorn hope in the storming of Seringapatam. He was a fighting man, ardent for warlike adventure, maimed with wounds, fevered by exposure, yet withal unlucky in promotion. He was full of affection for his family, and of generosity towards his friends. Despite the *res angusta domi* which often clings to unrewarded veterans, he was happy in his domestic life. His only sorrow was the indignant sense of the scant gratitude with which his country had regarded his services. Nevertheless he sent forth three of his sons for military careers in that same East where he himself had fought and bled,—of whom two rose to high rank and good emoluments.

But he placed them all in the service of the East India Company, which he hoped would prove a good master, and that hope was realised.

As a child, John Lawrence went with his parents from Richmond to Guernsey, thence to Ostend where the father commanded a Veteran Battalion during the Waterloo campaign, and thence soon after 1815 to Clifton near Bristol. During his childhood he suffered severely from an affection of the eyes, the very ailment which, as we shall see hereafter, overshadowed his declining years. From Clifton he went to a day-school at College Green in Bristol, walking daily over the breezy uplands that then separated the two places, in company with his brother Henry, his elder by five years. It would seem that according to the fashion of the schools of this class in those times, he received a rudimentary education with a harsh discipline. His home, being furnished with scanty means, must have been destitute of external amenities. But he enjoyed the care of one who, though forced by circumstances to be rigid, was a thoroughly good mother, and the tender thoughtfulness of his sister Letitia which he never forgot. He listened eagerly to his father's animated tales of war, as the veteran recounted

"the story of his life
From year to year, the battles, sieges, fortunes,
That he had passed . . .
Wherein he spoke of most disastrous chances,
Of moving accidents by flood and field,
Of hair-breadth 'scapes i' the imminent deadly breach."

Doubtless it was from his father's conversation in these days of childhood that he acquired the soldierly predilections which clung to him throughout his civil career. The receptive years of his boyhood up to twelve were thus spent in English surroundings, and amidst English scenery of an attractive character. Despite the whirl and worry of his after-life, he ever remembered the beautiful Clifton of his day—before the rocks were pierced for railway-tunnels or the valley spanned by a suspension-bridge. He loved the forest-clad heights, the limestone cliffs, the bed of the tidal Avon.

At twelve years of age he went to Foyle College close to Londonderry, to be under the care of the Reverend James Knox, his mother's brother. In this College were his brothers George and Henry, also Robert Montgomery, who was in future years to become to him the best of colleagues. Here he stayed during two years of great importance in the forming of his mind and disposition, as he breathed the air, imbibed the ideas, and gathered the associations of Ulster. At first, however, his ways were so much those of England that his companions called him "English John." The education which he there received was characteristic of the British type, for it tended rather to form and strengthen the character than to enlighten the intellect. The religious training, to which he was subjected, appears to have been somewhat too severely strict. Yet in combination with home influences and with natural impulses, it planted religion ineradicably deep in his heart. The recollection of it, however, rendered him adverse to formalism of any kind.

Foyle College as an educational institution has doubtless been much developed since his time. But the building and its precincts may now be seen almost exactly as they were when he was there. From the upper windows is the same prospect which he had of the Foyle estuary, and from the field where he played football is beheld a view of the historic city. As he used to stay there with his uncle during the holidays, he must have often walked round the terrace on the top of the well-kept walls, that still enclose the old citadel-town wherein the faith and freedom of the Protestants were sheltered during the storm of war in 1688-9. Here he found the historic memories preserved with wonderful tenacity. So he must have gazed at the Ship-Quay, the Water-gate as it once was, whither the relieving ships from England, after fighting their way up the Foyle, brought victuals for the long-suffering and famished garrison. He must have passed beneath the venerable bastions where the defenders repeatedly beat back the French soldiers of King James. He attended on Sundays divine service in the Cathedral which stood close to the fighting-ground during the defence, and where the bones of eminent defenders were interred. This, then, was just the place to be for him a *nutrix leonum*, and the meet nurse for a heroic child; as indeed it is the Saragossa of the British Isles. In after life his talk would oft revert to the Foyle as to him the queen of rivers. Forty years later, when at the summit of his greatness, he spoke publicly to his admirers in the Punjab about the memories of Londonderry, as nerving Britons in other lands to stubborn resistance.

At fifteen years of age he returned to England and went to a school kept at Wraxall Hall, near Bath, an Elizabethan structure with picturesque courtyards and orchards. It was comparatively near to his paternal home at Clifton, and in it were renewed those rural associations of English life which he had gathered in childhood. Shortly afterwards he was offered a civil appointment in the East India Company's service by a good friend, Mr. Hudlestone, who had already given appointments in the Company's military service to three of the elder brothers, one of whom was Henry. But he was minded to decline the civil appointment, then considered of all appointments the most desirable, and to ask for a military appointment instead. He would not regard the advice of his father, nor of his brother Henry, who had just returned from India on sick leave after hard service in the wars. The influence of his sister Letitia alone persuaded him to accept the civil appointment. Consequently at the age of seventeen he went to the East India Company's College at Haileybury near Hertford, and remained there for the appointed term of two years. There he heard lectures in political economy from Malthus, and in law from Empson, afterwards editor of the *Edinburgh Review*. The discipline was not specially strict, nor was the intellectual training severe; but as the Company maintained a highly qualified and distinguished staff of professors, he had educational opportunities of which he availed himself in a moderate or average degree only. He was a fairly good student, but was not regarded by his compeers as remarkable for learning or for prowess in games. His frame was tall and well knit but gaunt. His manner was reserved in public, sometimes tending to taciturnity, but vivacious and pleasant in private. As he had been thought to be English when in Ireland, so now when in England he was deemed to be somewhat Irish in his ways. In his case, as in many eminent cases, the temper and disposition were being fixed and settled, while the mental faculties were being slowly developed. The basis of his great character was being founded in silence. But his fondness for the rural side of English life must have been gratified to the full at College. He had not cultivated any architectural taste, and if he had, it would have been offended by the plainness even ugliness of the collegiate architecture; but his nature rejoiced in the surroundings of the College, the extensive woods reaching to the very gates, the outburst of vernal foliage, the singing birds in their leafy haunts, the open heath, the Rye House meadows, the waters of the Lea. He would roam with long strides in the meads and woodlands. Though not gifted with any æsthetic insight into the beauties of Nature, yet he would inwardly commune with her, and he had an observant eye for her salient features. Such things helped to establish a mind like his, and to temper it like pure steel for the battle of life.

He used to spend a part of his vacation in each year at the house of a friend at Chelsea, before returning to his home at Clifton. Having passed through College he spent four months in England, in order to have the companionship of Henry on the voyage out to India. He sailed in September 1829, being nineteen years old, in a vessel bound for Calcutta by the route round the Cape of Good Hope.

At a later stage in his life, some analysis will be given to show how far he partook of the several elements in our composite national character, English, Scotch and Irish. It may suffice here to state that for all these years his nurture, bringing up, and education generally, had been English, with the important exception of the two years which he spent at Londonderry. Whatever Scotch or Irish proclivities he may have possessed, and they will be considered hereafter, no son of England, of his age, ever left her shores more imbued than he with her ideas, more loyal to her principles, more cognisant of her strength or weakness, of her safety or danger, of her virtues or failings.

CHAPTER III

THE DELHI TERRITORY

1829-1846

John Lawrence, in company with his elder brother Henry, entered in 1829 upon his new life, beginning with a five months' voyage through the Atlantic and Indian Oceans. On this voyage he suffered severely from sea-sickness, and the suffering was protracted over several weeks. This must have aggravated any constitutional tendency to nervous irritability in his head. He landed at Calcutta in February, 1830, just when the cool season was over and the weather was growing warmer and warmer till it attained the heat of early summer. Then he passed through the rainy period of midsummer, which in those latitudes always had a depressing effect on him as on many others. He was an ordinarily good student in the College of Fort William—the official name whereby the stronghold of Calcutta is called. He mixed but little in the society of the capital, and pined for his English home, fancying that poverty there would be better than affluence in the East; he even allowed himself to be dominated by this sort of home-sickness, for the first and last time in his life. However, after sojourning for a few months in Calcutta, and passing the examination in the vernacular of Upper India, he asked for and obtained an appointment at Delhi, partly because his brother Henry was serving in the Artillery at Kurnal in that neighbourhood, partly also because the far-off frontier had a fascination for him as for many others. In those days a journey from Calcutta to Delhi (now accomplished by railway within three days) often occupied nearly three months by boat on the Ganges; but by travelling in a palanquin he traversed the distance, about eleven hundred miles, within three weeks.

Arrived at Delhi, in 1830, he felt that happy revulsion of thought and sentiment which is well known to many who have passed through similar circumstances. He had not only landed on a strange and distant shore, but had advanced many hundred miles into the interior of the country. He had thus, so to speak, cut his cables and cast away home-sickness, treasuring the memory of the former existence in the sunniest corner of his heart, but bracing and buckling himself to the work of the new existence. This work of his, too, was varied and intensely human in its interests. Its nature was such as made him anxious to learn, and yet the learning was extraordinarily hard at first. His dormant energies were thus awakened, as he dived deep into the affairs of the Indian people, listened to their petitions, guarded their rights, collected the taxes, watched the criminal classes, traced out crime, regulated the police. The work was in part sedentary, but it also afforded him healthy exercise on foot and on horseback, as he helped in supervising the streets, the drains, the roads, and the municipal institutions of all sorts in a great city and its neighbourhood.

He was, moreover, impressed deeply by imperial Delhi itself as one of the most noteworthy cities in the world, and as

"The lone mother of dead empires."

The matchless palace of the Great Mogul overhanging the river Jumna, the hall of audience, the white marble mosque, a veritable pearl of architecture, the great city mosque, probably the finest place of worship ever raised by Moslem hands, the ruins outside the walls of several capitals belonging to extinct dynasties, doubtless affected his imagination in some degree. But he was too much pre-occupied by work to regard these things as they would be regarded by artists or antiquarians. Nevertheless his native keenness of observation served him well even here, for he would describe the structural merits of these noble piles, the clean cutting of the red-sandstone and the welding together of the massive masonry. He was more likely to observe fully the geographical situation which gave commercial and political importance to the city in many ages, and preserved it as a capital throughout several revolutions. In the intervals of practical business he must have noticed the condition of the Great Mogul, whom the British Government then maintained as a phantom sovereign in the palace. But he could not have anticipated the position of fell activity into which this very *roi fainèant* was fated to be thrust some twenty-seven years later. It will be seen hereafter that the local knowledge which he thus gained of Delhi, served him in good stead during the most critical period of his after-life.

In 1834 he was placed in temporary charge of the district of Paniput, in a vast plain that stretches along the western bank of the Jumna. His being after only four years' service entrusted, as acting Magistrate and Collector, with the command of a district containing some thousands of square miles and some hundreds of thousands of inhabitants, was a proof of the early reputation he had won as a capable officer and well-informed administrator. At Paniput he controlled, as a superior, much the same work as that which he had performed as a subordinate at Delhi. That which he had learnt by laborious self-instruction on a smaller scale, he was now to practise on a larger. The area being extensive, and rapidity of movement being essential to the maintenance of a personal control over affairs, he used to ride on horseback over his district from end to end. Every arduous or dangerous case, fiscal or criminal, he would keep in his own hands; though even in these early days he trusted his subordinates when trustworthy, and made them do their duty as he did his. He did not, indeed, adorn all that he touched, but he stamped on it the mark of individuality. The natives soon learnt to regard him as the embodiment of British justice. The various sections of the population, the evil-disposed or the industrious, the oppressor or the oppressed, the suppliant for redress or the hardened wrong-doer,—all in their respective ways felt his personality. The good officers in India live, move and have their being among the people, and such was his daily routine. He could not fail, moreover, to be moved by the historic traditions of Paniput—the scene of the Mahabhârat, that antique epic of the Hindoos; the victory of the young Akber, the first of the Great Moguls; the Persian invasion under Nâdir Shah; the rout of the Mahrattas under Ahmed Shah the Afghan: especially must the tragic and touching incidents of the Mahratta disaster have appealed to susceptibilities such as his.

In these days he practised himself much in horsemanship, becoming a strong rider and a good judge of horses; it was truly to be said of him *gaudet equis canibusque.* He was a keen observer of steers and heifers, of bullocks for draught and plough. Being fond of animals generally, he studied their breeding, nurture and training, their temper, habits and capabilities. Though a stranger to botany as a science, he knew the local names of every tree and plant. He had a discriminating eye for the varieties of soil, the qualities of growing crops, the faults and merits of husbandry. Though not versed in the theory of economic science, he had an insight into the causes affecting the rise and fall of prices, the interchange of commodities, the origin and progress of wealth, the incidence of taxation. He had hardly, indeed, mastered the technicalities of finance, yet he had a natural bent for figures, and was a financier almost by instinct.

This was the spring-tide of his public life when he was bursting forth into vigour of body, soaring in spirit, and rejoicing like a young lion in healthy strength. Then, too, he was able to withstand the climate all the year round. For although in summer the sky was as brass, the earth as iron, the wind as a blast from a furnace, still in winter the marching in tents was salubrious, the breeze invigorating, the temperature delicious by day, and the air at night frosty.

After an incumbency of three years at Paniput he was transferred to Gurgaum, a district south of Delhi. There his work was the same as that already described, only somewhat harder, owing to the lawless and intractable habits of some classes among the inhabitants, and because of drought which visited and distressed that region. Then in 1838 he was appointed Settlement-Officer of Etawah, a district south-east of Delhi between the Ganges and the Jumna. In technical or official language, his settlement-work included the whole scope of landed affairs, in the most comprehensive as well as in the minutest sense,—the assessment of that land-tax, which is the main burden of the peasantry and the prime resource of the State—the cadastral survey of every field in every village or parish—the adjudication of all disputes regarding the rights, interests and property in land—the registration of landed tenures. His duty herein was, of all duties which can be entrusted to a man in India, the one of most interest and importance, the one which penetrates deepest into the national life, the one for which the Government always chooses its most promising officers. This duty, moreover, universally attractive to the best men throughout India, had for him especial charms in the districts between the Ganges and the Jumna. For here he found, in all their pristine and unimpaired vigour, those Village Communities which have survived the shocks of war and revolution, and have engaged the thoughts of jurists and philosophers. His business was to guard the innate and indestructible energy of these ancient communities, to adapt their development to the wants of the present time, to fence round their privileges and responsibilities with all the forms of a civilized administration. The experience thus gained was to him of unspeakable value in the most arduous passages of his after life. But though he entered with all his heart and mind into this work, he felt the district itself to be dull and distasteful after Delhi and Paniput, and this feeling shows how the antique splendour of the former and the historic traditions of the latter had affected his imagination. He could no longer live contentedly unless amidst his surroundings there were something grand for his mind to feed upon. However grateful he may have felt to Etawah for the experience it had given him, he never looked back on the place with pleasure. One melancholy recollection abided with him, for it was here that he caught his first serious illness, a violent fever which rapidly reduced him to the verge of death. By an effort of nature he shook it off and rallied for a while. Then in the autumn of 1839 he glided, as an invalid in river-boats, down the Jumna and the Ganges to Calcutta. There he had a relapse of fever, and decided in the beginning of 1840 to proceed to England, being entitled to furlough after his active service of ten years. He arrived in England during June of that year.

The first act in the drama of his public life was thus concluded. He had done well, he had mastered the details of a difficult profession, in his own words he "had learnt his business." He was esteemed by his comrades and his superiors as a competent officer in all respects; beyond this, however, nothing more was said or thought of him at that time. All this has been and yet will be recorded of hundreds of British officers in India, before or after him, whose names are nevertheless not written in the roll of fame. *Vixere fortes ante Agamemnona multi:* indeed many men as good as he then was are now living and will still live. Furthermore, many officers have, in the course of their first ten years, shown more signs of genius, or talent, or statesmanlike accomplishments, than he had displayed up to this time. When he sailed from Calcutta for England in 1840 neither he himself nor his friends had, on a retrospect of his first ten years, formed any idea of the career which he was to run during his second ten years, and had never, even in day-dreams, caught a vision of the destiny which awaited him during his third ten years. The elements of his character were being gradually fused into granitic consistency. To him was applicable that British metaphor, which though familiar is never trite because the proofs of its truth are oft-recurring: the sturdy oak grows slowly, but in proportion to that slowness is the ultimate strength to bear the weight, withstand the strain and resist the storm.

Returning to England during the summer of 1840, he found the home of his youth at Clifton much altered. His father had passed away, his sister Letitia had married, but his mother remained to benefit by his affectionate assistance. Though his health was not re-established, yet his energy and spirits revived under the European skies, and his vivacity astonished both friends and acquaintances. He proceeded to Bonn, and stayed there for a time with his sister-in-law, the wife of George Lawrence who was in Afghanistan. Then he paid visits in England and travelled in Scotland and Ireland. In Donegal he was so fortunate as to meet Harriette, daughter of the Reverend Richard Hamilton, whom he married in August 1841, thus forming a union of the very happiest character. He proceeded to the continent of Europe on a wedding-tour, passing through Switzerland to Italy, and gathered notions, in his practical way, regarding the policy and strategy of ancient Rome. He particularly noticed the campaigns of Hannibal, to which he often alluded in after-life. But the Indian ailments partially reappeared in the malarious climate of the Roman campagna. At Naples, in the beginning of 1842, he received news of the disasters at Caubul and hurried home to England, sorely anxious regarding the captivity of his brother George amidst the Afghans. In London he had a grave relapse of illness, but was sufficiently recovered by the autumn to start for India by the overland route, after bidding a last farewell to his mother.

During his sojourn in England of little more than two years, he left upon every one who conversed with him a marked impression of his originality, elasticity, animated conversation, brightness of spirit and physical force. Those who saw him only when he was well, little thought how suddenly he could become ill, and —erroneously, alas!—supposed him to be a man of abounding health as well as strength. None, however, foresaw his future greatness, or even predicted for him a career more useful than that which is run by the many able and zealous men who are found in the Indian service. This failure of prescience is the more remarkable, because his elder brother Henry had long been designated by admiring comrades as one of the heroes and statesmen of the future.

He landed with his wife at Bombay towards the end of 1842, and thus gained his first experience of Western India. Thence he travelled by palanquin, at the rate of thirty miles a day, over the eight hundred miles that separated him from Allahabad in the North-Western Provinces to which he officially belonged. In the beginning of 1843 he marched at the rate of ten miles a day in tents towards the Delhi territory, where he was thankful to find employment. The tent-life in the bracing winter-season of Upper India was very beneficial to him physically, and he resumed work amidst his early associations in good health. With his wife and young children he settled down to the routine of public life, and girded himself for the discharge of ordinary duties. At Kurnal, not far from Delhi, he made a searching and practical analysis of the causes which produced a malarious and disabling sickness among the troops stationed there. In 1844 he was appointed to the substantive post of Magistrate and Collector of Delhi. While holding this appointment he laid the foundation of his fortunes in public life. In November, 1845, he first met the Governor-General, Lord Hardinge, who passed through Delhi to join the army assembling near the Sutlej for the first Sikh war. His bearing, conversation and subsequent proceedings, made a lasting impression on the mind of the Governor-General, who ever afterwards spoke and wrote of him as the ideal of what a civil officer for India ought to be.

He soon justified by deeds the high estimate thus

formed respecting him, for he was charged with the duty of finding transport for the siege train with its heavy guns, stores and munitions from Delhi to the battlefields on the bank of the Sutlej; and this transport was to consist of four thousand carts with bullocks and drivers complete. He furnished a signal instance of the manner whereby in India the civil administration aids the army by providing transport in time of war. Such transport, in quantities adequate for the service, cannot be obtained without a really powerful organisation; during public emergency it can by law be forcibly impressed, but when thus collected it is likely to prove inefficient unless the civil authority makes such arrangements as may secure the contentment of those from whom the vehicles and the animals are hired: in this case his arrangements were practically perfect. Within a very short time he so managed that all the thousands of carts should be driven by their owners, who, for good hire, partly paid in advance, became willing to undertake the service. He despatched the long-extended train in complete order so that it arrived, without any straggling or deserting, without the failure of a man, a wheel or a bullock, in time for the battle of Sobraon. For the first time in his life a public service had been demanded from him of definite importance, requiring knowledge of the natives, aptitude for command and power of organisation. He at once stepped to the very front as if to the manner born. His capacity, too, was evinced in a large affair, wherein the Governor-General from personal experience was peculiarly qualified to adjudge the merit. So when, as a consequence of the war, the Trans-Sutlej

States were shorn from the Sikh kingdom and annexed to the British dominions, he was appointed by Lord Hardinge to be the Commissioner and Superintendent of the newly-acquired territory.

He quitted his command at Delhi early in 1846, never dreaming of the wonderful circumstances in which he was destined to resume it only eleven short years later in 1857. Those who reflect on the reserve force, the dormant capacity, the latent energy that existed within him, might imagine poetically the surging thoughts that made his breast heave as he drove or rode off from the bank of the Jumna with his face set towards the bank of the Sutlej. But such was not his manner; if he had leisure to meditate at all, he would have peered into the future with a modest even a humble look, anticipating the disappointments rather than the successes that might be in store for him. On his way, though at the most favourable season of the year, he was seized with a sharp attack of cholera. From that, however, he rallied quickly, and crossed the Sutlej in sufficiently good health, and with buoyant spirits.

CHAPTER IV

THE TRANS-SUTLEJ STATES

1846-1849

FROM the last preceding chapter it has been seen that in March, 1846, John Lawrence was appointed Commissioner of the territory, known officially as the Trans-Sutlej States, and geographically as the Jullandur Doab, containing thirteen thousand square miles and two and a half millions of inhabitants. He thus became prefect of this newly-annexed territory, which was placed not under any provincial Government but under the immediate administration of the Governor-General in Council. It was divided into three districts, with district officers who were to exercise power as great as that which he had possessed at Delhi, in some respects greater indeed, and he was in command of them all. He was at the head of what was then the frontier province of the empire, and under the eye of the Governor General. His foot was on the first step of the ladder which leads to greatness, but it was quite doubtful whether he would succeed in mounting any further steps. His temper was naturally masterful in that degree which is essential to any considerable achievements in human affairs. This quality in him had been fostered by his service at Delhi. It had the fullest play in his new province, which lay half at the base of the Himalayas and half within the mountains. Below the hills he found the territory fertile, the population sturdy, and the land with its inhabitants like plastic clay to be moulded by his hand. Old-standing wrongs were to be redressed, half-suppressed rights to be vindicated, tenures to be settled, crimes to be stamped out, order to be introduced not gradually but rapidly, law to be enforced in spirit if not in letter, an administration to be rough-hewn after civilised models, provincial finance to be managed; here, then, he was in his element. This was, probably, the happiest time of his whole life, and the most satisfactory portion of his long career. In after years he would recur to it wistfully, when troubled by other surroundings and beset by other circumstances. There he had quite his own way, and left his proper mark; for in a few months he laid broadly and deeply the foundations of good administration. Besides the civil business, there was other work demanding his care. The province contained not only the rich and peopled plain near the confluence of the Sutlej and the Beas, but also a Himalayan region extending northwards to Tibet and held by mountaineer chieftains; and he had to reduce this mountainous country also to reasonable obedience. The results he attained in six months, that is from March to August 1846, seem on a retrospect to be wonderful, and prove with what method as well as force, what steadiness as well as energy, what directness of aim, what adaptation of means to righteous purposes, he must have laboured. Throughout these affairs he was in direct and immediate relations with the Government of India from whom he received ample support. And he more than justified the confidence of the Governor-General, Lord Hardinge, who had selected him.

Though his new charge in the Trans-Sutlej States was distant not more than two hundred miles from his old charge at Delhi,—which for north-western India is a short distance—there was a change of scene. Around Delhi and Paniput he had seen scenery as flat as that of northern or south-eastern Europe in the basin, for instance, of the Elbe and the Oder or of the Don and the Volga. No mountain wall, no abrupt peak, no wooded eminence, broke for him the monotony of outline, or bounded his horizon which ran in a complete circle like the horizon at sea. But in the Trans-Sutlej States on a fine winter's morn, his northern horizon of the plains was bounded by a glittering wall of the snowy Himalayas, a sight which, when beheld by Europeans for the first time, so affects them that they instinctively raise their hats to the peerless mountains. Within the lower hills, which are outworks of the greater ranges, he rode up and down stony bridle-paths or across the sandy beds of summer-torrents, and gazed at hill-forts on stiff heights, or on castles like that of Kot-Kangra rising proudly from the midst of ravines with precipitous surroundings. Penetrating further northwards he reached mountains, with fir-woods bounded by snow, which reminded him of his Alpine tour only four years ago, and thought how short that interval was, and yet how much had happened to him within it. Though not specially sensitive to the beauties of Nature, he would yet dilate with something near enthusiasm on the vale of Dhurmsala, with its cultivated slopes, intersected by a net-work of artificial rivulets or murmuring brooks, and surrounded by forests of oak and pine, while above the scene there towered the everlasting snows that look down upon the transient littleness of man. But he lingered not in any scene, however glorious, for his heart was with the swarthy population under his charge in the hot and dusty plains below.

In August, 1846, he was called away to Lahore to act for his brother Henry as British Resident with the Regency of the Punjab. Here he had a fresh field of action, which though nominally new was yet one where his experience of native life enabled him to enter at once with full effect. He was temporarily the agent of the paramount British power in a Native State, torn by restless and incompatible factions, and possessing the *débris* of a warlike power that had been shattered by British arms in recent campaigns. He was, however, acting for his brother absent on leave, on whose lines he loyally worked. But though he had no chance of showing originality, he yet evinced capacity for that which in India is called political work, and which though cognate to, is yet distinct from, civil administration.

He resumed charge of his province, the Trans-Sutlej States, by the end of 1846, and consolidated his work there during the first half of 1847. But in August of that year he was again called to act for Henry at Lahore, who had proceeded on sick leave to England. By this time a further arrangement had been made, placing the supervision of the Punjab, during the minority of the Native Prince, under the British Resident. Consequently during this his second incumbency at

Lahore he enjoyed a largely extended authority, and the evidence he gave of capacity increased together with his opportunities. He remained at Lahore from the middle of 1847 to the spring of 1848, when he made over his political charge to Sir Frederick Currie, and returned to his province in the Trans-Sutlej States. During this time his friend Lord Hardinge had been succeeded by Lord Dalhousie as Governor-General. Hardly had he resumed the civil command of his province when the rebellion broke out at Mooltan in the southern Punjab, and spread over the whole country west of Lahore. During the events which followed, throughout 1848 and up to the spring of 1849, and which have been regarded by history as constituting the second Punjab War, he held his provincial command with characteristic vigour. The rebellious fire in the Punjab sent many sparks into the inflammable materials in the hill-districts of his jurisdiction. Newly subdued chiefs, occupying mountainous territories, showed their teeth, and there was anxiety for the safety of Kot-Kangra, the famous hill-fort which was the key of the surrounding country; but in an instant he seemed to be ubiquitous. With scanty resources in troops, and with hastily raised levies, he struck blows which prevented insurrection from making head. Throughout the war his Trans-Sutlej province, occupying a critical position between the elder British dominions and the Punjab, was kept well in hand.

In the beginning of 1849 he repaired to Lahore to confer with Henry, who had come back from England and resumed charge of the Residency. He remained in close communication with his brother till after the termination of the war by the battle of Gujerat in February of that year. In March he went on his brother's behalf to Ferozepur, whither the Governor-General, Lord Dalhousie, had come in order to determine the fate of the Punjab. There he met Lord Dalhousie for the first time, and discussed with him the principal matters connected with the annexation of the country—not the policy of annexing, for that had really been determined, but rather the best way of carrying that measure into effect. The conference being verbal and confidential, the substance cannot be given; but he certainly advised the Governor-General that if annexation was to be decreed there was not a moment to be lost, for in the first place the spring crops, the main sources of the land revenue, were ripening for harvest, and the Government interests would be sacrificed by delay; and in the second place, the hot weather was coming on apace, and very few weeks remained wherein the British officers could possibly move about and establish order in the country. This valuable and withal characteristic advice of his must have carried due weight with Lord Dalhousie.

The Punjab being annexed immediately afterwards, he was appointed a member of the Board of Administration of which Henry was President. The Board was constituted for managing the country, though the powers of the Government were reserved for the Governor-General in Council; but its functions were comprehensive and he was an important member of it.

He was now on the threshold of Anglo-Indian greatness, with nineteen years' standing in the service, including two years of furlough in England. For some time his health had been fairly good; he was in the zenith of strength and in the prime of life; he was happy in his domestic circumstances; he was as yet on good terms officially with his eminent brother Henry as he ever was privately. He had shown himself to be perfectly equipped for civil administration, competent for extended command, able in dealing with political contingencies, active in the field as well as laborious in the cabinet, prompt in suppressing disturbance, equal to grave emergency. Nevertheless, he had not up to this time conceived any idea of a great future being in store for him. He had seen men of signal power, whom he reverently regarded, leave India without reward or external honour, although their fame might live for generations in the hearts of many millions, and he hardly expected any different issue for himself.

At the present stage the main points may be reviewed in his public character which by this time had been cast in its lasting mould. The basis and framework of his nature assuredly belonged to what is familiarly known as the British type. The earliest influences brought to bear upon him had been English absolutely, and the effect, thus produced at the most impressionable age, abided with him to the end. Later on, however, a quality developed itself in him which is not especially English, namely caution. This he derived, no doubt, from his mother's Scottish blood. He was an extremely cautious man, and obeyed the dictates of caution up to the utmost reasonable limit. Whenever he acted in a dashing and daring manner—as he sometimes had to do—it was only after a cool, even though a rapid, review of diverse considerations. He thought that as a race the

English are incautious, even impatient in time of energetic action, and apt to feel too secure and self-sufficing in time of quiet. When preparing instructions for a possible emergency, he would often say that they must be so framed as to guard against the over-impetuous disposition of our countrymen in the presence of danger. As a cognate quality to caution, he had forethought in the highest degree. In all considerable affairs he habitually disciplined his mind to think out the probable or possible future, to perceive beforehand what might or might not happen, to conjure up the contingencies which might arise, to anticipate the various turns which events might take. This faculty must, indeed, be possessed more or less by all who achieve anything great in public life; but probably few men ever possessed it in a higher degree than he. For ill-digested policy, or hastily judged action, or inconsiderate rashness, he had nothing but pity and contempt. With such a temperament as this he would willingly, indeed anxiously, listen to all that could be said on the several sides of every question, collate the opinions of others, and gather local knowledge before making up his own mind. After that, however, his mind would be made up decisively without further delay, and would be followed by action with all his might. Thus he became essentially a man of strong opinions, and was then self-reliant absolutely. The test of a first-rate man, as distinguished from ordinary men, is the fitness to walk alone; that was his favourite expression, meaning doubtless the exercise of undivided responsibility. Thus he was masterful in temperament. He would yield obedience readily to those whom he was bound to obey, but would quickly chafe if the orders he received were couched in inconsiderate terms. He would co-operate cordially with those from whom he had no right to expect more than co-operation; but he always desired to be placed in positions where he would be entitled to command. Though not thirsting for power in the ordinary sense of the term, he never at any stage of his career felt that he had power enough for his work and his responsibilities. He certainly complained often on this score. His confidence in the justice of his own views was complete, because he knew that he had thought them out, and was conscious of being gifted with the power of thinking. Still he was not aggressively dogmatic, nor uncharitable to contrary opinions on the part of others, but rather forbearing. He would modestly say that these opinions of theirs should be respected, but his own view was formed, and he must act upon it. Hesitancy might be desirable during the stage of deliberation, but was not, in his mind, permissible when once the conclusions had been reached, for then it must give place to promptitude in action.

He had one faculty which is characteristic of the best English type, namely, the power of judging evenly and calmly in regard to the merits or demerits of those with whom he had to deal. Without undue predilection he would note the faults or failings of those who on the whole had his admiration. Equally without prejudice he would make allowance for the weakness of those whom he reprobated, and would recollect any countervailing virtue. He was ready to condone errors in those who were zealous for the public service. But to those who were lacking in desire for the performance of duty he would show no consideration, notwithstanding any gifts or accomplishments which they might possess. In holding a just balance between virtues and faults in others, or estimating with discrimination the diverse moral and intellectual qualities of those who were responsible to him, he has rarely, if ever, been surpassed. It almost necessarily follows that he was a keen observer and an accurate judge of character in all with whom he came in contact. He was inclined to believe more in men than in measures. Almost any plan, he would say, will answer with good men to execute it, with such men even an inferior system will succeed; but with bad or indifferent men to work it, the best system will fail.

While the basis of his disposition was British, still there was in him an Irish element. His heart was with Ulster, and in his hardest times he would recur to the defence of Londonderry. He was often humorous, vivacious and laughter-loving, to a degree which is not usual with Britons of so rough and hard a fibre as his. He was frequently grave and silent; his temper, too, though very good in reality, was not mild, and occasionally might seem to be irascible; nevertheless when at his ease, or off his guard, he would relax at once into smiles and witticisms. If wrapped up in preoccupation of thought—as was but too often the case—he must needs be serious. But if not preoccupied, he would look forth upon the world around him, men, things, animals and objects generally, with a genial desire to gain amusement from them all, and to express that amusement in racy terms to any friend or companion who might be with him. As he moved along a thoroughfare of traffic or the streets of a city, his talk sparkled like a hill-stream flowing freshly over a stony bed. His wit was abundantly seasoned by the use of metaphor. His figures of speech were drawn not only from his native West but from the East of his adoption. His *repertoire* and vocabulary were thus enriched from Oriental resources which abound in imagery. He had in early years acquired not a scholar-like but a competent knowledge of Persian. Thus he was able to apply the similes, the tropes, the quirks of that flowery language to passing objects in a manner which moved everyone European or Native to laughter. He had an amazing memory for tales of real life, in the East chiefly, and these he would on occasion narrate in a vivid or graphic style.

Beneath a rough-hewn exterior there flowed an undercurrent of gentleness and tenderness which he reserved for his home. In his domestic life he was thoroughly happy, and fortunate beyond the average lot of mankind. This had a quieting and softening effect upon him amidst the distraction and excitement of active life. Never having studied art of any kind, or paid any attention to music and painting, he would not idealize anything, nor take an artistic view of the grand and glorious objects in Nature that often met his eye. But if such an object affected military or political combinations—as for instance a precipitous defile, a bluff headland, a treacherous river-passage, a rockbound ravine—then he would describe it with eloquent, even poetic, illustrations.

He had by nature an acute and far-reaching eyesight, which, however, in middle life became impaired by excessive reading both in print and manuscript. But this reading of his ranged for the most part over official papers only. He read but little of literature generally,—that little, however, would be in the heroic mould, something that related to the struggles of ancient Rome, or her contest with Carthage, or the marches of Alexander the Great, or the stirring episodes of Irish history, or the English policy of Cromwell, or the travels of Livingstone. His classical lore extended to Latin only; he knew but little of Greek and rarely alluded to the efforts of Athens or Sparta. To the Book of books he turned daily; with its more than mortal eloquence he had by reverent study familiarised himself. As a steadfast member of the Church of England, he had passages from the Church Services read to him constantly. For all other books, too, he would, if possible, find some one to read aloud, being anxious to spare his eyes. Had he not lived always in official harness, he would have been adventurous, for he loved to collate and describe the adventures of others. Had his leisure sufficed, he would have been a reader of the fine romances with which our literature is adorned. But he could only enjoy a few selected works, and his choice fell chiefly on the novels of Walter Scott. The finest of these would be read out to him in evenings at home, because, among other reasons, they reminded him of his visit to Scotland in 1841.

His pen was that of a ready as well as a busy writer, though in all his life he never wrote a line of literary composition. His writing was either official or what is called demi-official. In the Delhi territory his extensive correspondence was mainly in the vernacular, for which native amanuenses were employed. In the Trans-Sutlej States it was largely in English, and had to be conducted by his own hand. In the still higher offices which he was now to fill, the services of secretaries are available, and he needed seldom to write long despatches or minutes. Some few reports, however, he did write, and these are marked throughout by a clear, straightforward and forcible style; the salient features in a situation, the points in the character of a person, the elements in a political combination, being sketched offhand in a simple but telling manner, and even with some degree of picturesque effect. The excellence in these reports of his, few and far between, attracted Lord Dalhousie's notice. He never was content with communicating his views and wishes officially, but would usually reinforce his public instructions with private letters. He wrote privately to all officers of importance whom he wished to impress with his sentiments. He encouraged them to write to him and he invariably answered their letters. Distance, separation and other circumstances, render it necessary to employ writing more largely in India than in any other country, and certainly his writing was enormous in quantity as well as varied in interest. Copies were kept of his countless letters, filling many volumes. Still every letter was short and decisive, for he tried to spare words and to array his meaning in the most succinct form. But his extant correspondence is almost entirely of a public nature. The series of his private letters to his sister Letitia is stated to have been deliberately destroyed. At the time now under reference the electric telegraph had not been introduced into India; after its introduction he seized on this new means of communication, the brevity of which suited his temperament. In the years between 1856 and 1859 probably no man in the world sent off so many telegrams as he. He had no practice whatever for public speaking in English, but he could address a limited audience of Natives, either civil or military, in the vernacular with point and effect.

Though never courting applause, and ready to incur odium for the sake of duty, he was not indifferent to the good opinion of others. With all his reserve, he was more sensitive to sympathy or to estrangement than was, perhaps, commonly supposed. He had not, during the middle stage of his career, much to do with the Press or the organs of public opinion. He was strict in demanding from all men a more than ordinary standard of work and of exertion, setting an example by his own practice. He was guarded, even chary, in awarding praise; still for real desert he always had the good word which was spoken in season and was valued accordingly. He never forgot that by training and profession he was a Covenanted Civil Servant, first of the East Indian Company and then of the Crown. No member of the Covenanted Civil Service was ever more jealous of its traditions, more proud of its repute, than he. No officer ever laboured harder than he to learn civil business proper, as distinguished from all other kinds of business. Yet he was by instinct and temper a soldier, and was ever studying martial affairs or acquiring military knowledge. He would familiarly speak of himself as the son of a soldier and the brother of three soldiers. Herbert Edwardes of Peshawur, who knew him well and was a competent judge on such a subject, wrote of him as a man of real military genius.

The crowning grace of his rough-hewn character was a simplicity, the genuine result of single-mindedness. The light of religion shed a gentle radiance over his whole life and conversation. For him, too, the path of religious duty was brightened by his wife's example.

The habits of his daily life are worth mentioning, as they were originally and as they became afterwards. Up to the present time, 1849, he always rose early, and by sunrise all the year round was on horseback or on foot. Returning home before the sun was high in the heaven, he did some of his best work indoors before breakfast. This work would be continued all day till late in the afternoon, when he would be again out of doors until nightfall. After that he would refrain from work and retire early. As he had duty out of doors as well as indoors, this routine was very suitable to the public service and preserved the *mens sana in corpore sano.* It was kept up by him after 1849 whenever he was on the march or in camp, for several months in every year, though he would sometimes drive in a gig or a carriage where formerly he would have ridden or walked. But it became gradually intermitted when he was in quarters, that is when he was stationary under a roof, owing to illness and to the consequent diminution of physical force. He would then go out in the early morning if there was anything to be done, such as the inspecting of public works or the visiting of institutions. But if he did not move out, still he would be at work in his study very soon after sunrise at all seasons. At no time, however, did he fail to be in the open air at eventide when the sun was low. He was temperate and abstemious, and he advocated moderation, believing that in a hot climate the European constitution is apt to suffer not only from the use of stimulants but also from excess of animal food.

The mode of his work changed as years rolled on. Up to this time, 1849, he had to listen and talk more, to read and write less; and for his constitution this was the best. But after 1849, the process became reversed by degrees, and he had to read and write very much, which was detrimental to him. In official diligence and regularity, distributed evenly over the whole range and course of business, he has never been excelled and rarely equalled. In the power of despatching affairs of all sorts great and small, ordinary and emergent, in perfect style for all practical purposes, he was a master hand. When he had risen to high office with a secretariat staff at his disposal, his ordinary method was in this wise. As he read a long despatch or reference he inscribed short marginal notes as his eye passed on from paragraph to paragraph; or if the reference was a short one in a folded letter, he would in the fewest words endorse his opinion on the outer fold. From the marginal notes or from the endorsements his secretaries would prepare the despatches in draft, and the drafts in all important cases would be submitted for his approval. The number of despatches which within a few hours would come back from him with his marks on them to the secretariat was astonishing. Again in the largest matters he had a masterly manner of explaining verbally to a secretary the substance of what was to be written and touching on the various points. He would thus indicate orally in a few minutes a course of argument which must for the secretary occupy some hours in order to express it all in writing. But though no statesman ever knew better how to make a full use of the secretariat, still he bore even in writing his full share, and his secretaries entirely joined in the admiration felt for him by the world at large. Indeed they esteemed him the most because they knew him the best. Though no longer brought into hourly intercourse with the Natives all day, he yet kept up the habit of conversing with them, of receiving visits from them, of listening to petitions, of gathering information even from the humblest regarding the hopes and fears, the joys and sorrows of the people. While anxious to consult the views and wishes of the upper classes, he was resolved that the industrial masses of the population should be cared for. He dissented from the opinion which has been sometimes held that gratitude finds no place in the Oriental vocabulary. Give the Natives something to be grateful for, he would say, and they will shew gratitude fast enough.

His appearance was much in accord with the character which has thus been sketched. He was above the middle height, with a broad and powerful frame, a forward-gait and a strong stride; though, alas, care, labour and sickness, as years rolled on, reduced the frame and lessened its activity. His head was massive, his brow open, his face lined and furrowed, his eye grey and piercing but somewhat small, his hair originally dark but slightly silvered even in middle life, his complexion somewhat sunburnt. His expression was that of majestic simplicity, but when in repose he had an air of solemnity. His voice in ordinary talk was neither loud nor deep, but under strong emotion it could resound powerfully. The most noteworthy feature was his mouth; for though it might be closely set while the mind was working, yet in moments of ease it was mobile, and constantly opened with a natural grace for smiles, or laughter, or the play of wit and fancy. Withal he was of that rugged type, sometimes termed Cromwellian by his friends, which affords some of the fittest subjects for the painter or the sculptor.

CHAPTER V

PUNJAB BOARD OF ADMINISTRATION

1849-1853

In the preceding chapters we have followed the development of John Lawrence's character amidst his personal surroundings, without dwelling upon the condition of the provinces in which he served. But in this chapter and in the succeeding chapter, we must note specifically the status and the progress of the great Province in which he is engaged. He is now in a commanding position, certainly; but the crisis of his life is not yet come. Against that crisis he is unconsciously to make ready himself and his province. He is to set his house in order straightway, because on such ordering must depend the ability of the Punjab for doing that which it was required to do eight years later. Upon that supreme ability, on the part of him and his at the crucial moment, hung the fate of British dominion in the most important part of the Indian empire. The war-ship of the Punjab is now in sight, that ship which is not only to brave the battle and the breeze, bearing her own wounds, but is also to tow her wounded, battered, half-disabled consort into the haven of safety. It is well, then, for us to see how she was designed, welded compactly, built in water-tight compartments, launched and sent to sea.

Further, though John Lawrence has a commanding position, he is not yet in sole command of the Punjab administration. It is necessary to recount the circumstances whereby he came to be vested locally with that single and individual authority which he wielded with immense effect, during the crisis to be described hereafter.

It has been seen, then, that the Board of Administration for the Punjab was constituted by Lord Dalhousie in March, 1849. Henry Lawrence was President of the Board, and John was his colleague. A third member was also appointed, but after a short time he went away. The successor was Robert Montgomery, who had been the schoolfellow of the two Lawrences at Foyle College and a friend to them both equally. He was the one man in whom each of them would confide, when they differed with one another. Henry would, in his differences with John, open his heart to Montgomery. John too would speak of Montgomery as his *bhai* or brother. In addition to sterner qualities, the signal display of which will be seen hereafter, Montgomery possessed all those qualities which are needed for a peacemaker and mediator. His position at the Board, then, in conjunction with the two Lawrences was most fortunate. He had the art of making business move smoothly, rapidly and pleasantly. For the two brothers did, as will be explained presently, differ not privately nor fraternally but officially. When differences arise between two such eminent persons as these, each of them must naturally have his own adherents, especially as Henry was a military Officer in Staff employ and John a Covenanted Civil Servant, or in simpler phrase the former was a soldier and the latter a civilian. Consequently something like party spirit arose which never was very acute and which has perhaps, under the influence of time, died away. To attempt any description of Henry Lawrence here would be to travel beyond the purpose of this book. But he cannot, even here, be wholly dissociated from the present account of John's career. In order to avoid the semblance of passing over or disparaging Henry, it may suffice now to state briefly and summarily what he was in 1849, and what he continued to be up to his untimely and lamented death in 1857. This may preferably be done now, before the necessity arrives for explaining the difference (respecting certain public affairs only) which arose between him and his brother.

Henry Lawrence, then, was a man of talent, of poetic temper, of sentiment, of meteoric energy, and of genius. Though destitute of external gifts and graces, he yet possessed qualities which were inner gifts and graces of the soul, and which acted powerfully upon men. From his spirit an effulgence radiated through an ever-widening circle of friends and acquaintances. Being truly lovable, he was not only popular but beloved both among Europeans and Natives. He was generous almost to a fault, and compassionately philanthropic. Indeed his nature was aglow with the enthusiasm of humanity. As might perhaps be expected, he was quick-tempered and over-sensitive. His conversational powers were brilliant, and his literary aptitude was considerable, though needing more culture for perfect development. His capacity for some important kinds of affairs was vast. In emergencies demanding a combination of military, political and civil measures he has never been surpassed in India. He was mortally wounded by a shell when at the height of his usefulness. Had he lived to confront national danger in its extremity, he would have proved himself to be one of the ablest and greatest men that ever went forth from the shores of England to vindicate the British cause in the East. As a civil governor he had some but not all of the necessary qualifications. He had knowledge, wide and deep, of the Indian people, sympathy with their hopes and fears, tenderness for their prejudices, an abiding sense of justice towards them and an ardent desire for their welfare. He had that mastery of topographical details which is very desirable in administration. He was zealous in promoting public improvement and material development. He had a clear insight into character, and knew perfectly how to select men after his own heart. These he would attach to himself as disciples to a master. But in a civil capacity he had several defects. Though he could despatch affairs spasmodically, he was unsystematic almost unmethodical in business. Though he might make a system succeed in a certain way while he and his *alumni* lived or remained present to exercise control, yet he would not have been able to carry measures of complexity and establish them on foundations to stand the test of time. Moreover he was not, and never could have become, a financier; indeed he was not sufficiently alive to financial considerations. Great things have indeed been sometimes accomplished by statesmen and by nations in disregard, even in contravention, of financial principles; yet he might as a civil governor, if uncontrolled, have run the State ship into danger in this respect. Then being by nature impetuous, and possessed with ideas in themselves noble, he was hard to be controlled.

This short digression is necessary, in order to do justice to a great and good man who is indissolubly connected with the subject of this book.

The Board of Administration, then, composed of these three men began, founded and built up an administration, which lasted without interruption till 1857, and was the most brilliant that has ever been seen in India. They had co-ordinate authority, and ostensibly acted in solidarity. But among themselves there was a division of labour in ordinary matters: that is to say, Henry took the political and military departments, John the financial and fiscal including the land settlements, Montgomery the judicial and the police; while on important matters pertaining to any department whatever, each of the three members had his voice, the majority of course prevailing. If figuratively Henry was the heart of the Board and Montgomery its arm, then John was veritably its backbone.

Accordingly John had his headquarters permanently fixed at Lahore, and he straightway proceeded to build himself a home there. He found it to be really a Mahommedan city, the ancient capital of Moslem dynasties from Central Asia, which had been retained by the Sikhs as their political centre, while their national and religious centre was at Amritsar, some thirty miles off. Its noble mosques, its fortress-palace, its imperial tombs, must have brought back to his mind the associations of Delhi. At this time, 1849-50, he was in full health and strength; alas, these were the last years of unimpaired comfort physically that he was ever to enjoy. Those who saw in after years the iron resolution and the energy which even sickness could not subdue, can imagine the magnificent vigour he threw at this time into the work of pacifying a much disturbed province, reducing it to order and calling forth its resources.

There is not space here to describe the territories under the Board of Administration. Suffice it to say that the British territories comprised the Cis and Trans-Sutlej States and the Punjab proper, or the basins of the Indus and its affluents, together with Native States on the east of the Sutlej, and in the Himalayan region, including the famous valley of Cashmere. The name Punjab, a Persian word denoting five-waters, refers to this river-system. The total area of all kinds amounted to one hundred and thirty-five thousand square miles, and the population to just twenty millions; both area and population being exclusive of the Cashmere kingdom. The climate is much the same as that of the Delhi territory already described, except that the winter is sharper and longer while the autumn is more feverish. The people, consisting chiefly of Moslems and Sikhs, was quite the strongest, manliest and sturdiest that the British had ever had to deal with in India. On two sides the country was bordered by British districts, and on one side by the Himalayas. So far, then, the circumstances were favourable. But on the front or western side, the border touched on Afghanistan for eight hundred miles, and was the most arduous frontier in the Eastern empire.

The administration, known as that of the Lawrences in the Punjab, was in its day famous throughout India, and those engaged in it were too busy to reflect upon its characteristics. But after the lapse of a whole generation, or more than thirty years, a retrospect of that epoch may be calmly taken in a summary divested of technicalities.

In 1852 the Board caused a report to be drawn up of their administration; which is known in Indian history as "The First Punjab Report." But it would not now suffice to state, in the words of this document, that internal peace had been preserved, the frontier guarded, and the various establishments of the State organised; that violent crime had been repressed, the penal law executed, and prison discipline enforced; that civil justice had been administered in a simple and popular manner; the taxation readjusted and the revenue system reformed; that commerce had been set free, agriculture fostered, the national resources developed, and plans for future improvement projected.

Some further explanation is needed to indicate the true position of the Board in the administrative annals of India. For, together with due acknowledgment of the zeal, capacity and knowledge, evinced in all these cardinal matters, it must yet be remembered that these are the very matters which have always been undertaken either promptly or tardily, and with more or less of success, by every administration in every province that has within this century been added to the Indian empire. Nevertheless the Punjab Board had an unsurpassed, perhaps even an unequalled merit; and it is well to note exactly in what that merit consisted; for through this merit alone was the province subdued, pacified and organised in time, so as to be prepared for the political storm which it was destined to confront within eight short years. Time indeed was an essential element in the grand preparation. Upon this preparedness, as we shall see hereafter, the issue was to depend, either for victory or for wide-spread disaster, to the British cause in Northern India.

Now the Board showed its statesmanship because it did straightway, almost out of hand, with comparative completeness, that which others had done elsewhere by degrees at first and sometimes incompletely at last. To enjoin authoritatively the carrying out of such measures and to describe them when carried out may be comparatively easy; but to carry them out all at once in a new province under strange conditions, and in the teeth of innumerable obstacles, is hard indeed. Yet this is what the Board actually accomplished. It set to work simultaneously upon varied and intricate subjects, which other authorities elsewhere had been content, or else had been forced, to undertake by degrees, or piecemeal one by one according to opportunities in the course of years. But to the Board every week was precious and every month was eventful. It thus managed to effect, in a short span of years, as much as had been effected elsewhere in two or more decades. It is indeed but too easily conceivable that work done with rapid energy may result in imperfections injuring the effect of the whole. But the Board's operations were masterly in conception, thorough in foundation, business-like in details. So far the work has never been excelled and seldom rivalled in other provinces, either before or since that era.

On the other hand, the Board enjoyed several advantages which were almost unique. Its genius was partly shown in this that such advantages were seized, grasped tightly and turned to the best use. A mass of valuable experience has been garnered up amidst the older provinces, and was available for guidance or encouragement. Thus many projects became demonstrably practicable as well as desirable, which might otherwise have been disputable or untenable. The Governor-General, Lord Dalhousie, having annexed the Punjab, had justly the strongest motives for ensuring speedy success for the administration of the province. He had at his disposal the imperial resources, and these were consequently placed at the disposal of the Board to an extent which has never been seen in any other Indian province. Again, there was something in the strategic position, the historic repute, and in the internal circumstances of the Punjab, to attract the idiosyncrasy of the Anglo-Indian Services; therefore able and aspiring men were willing to volunteer for service there, even with all its risks and hardships. Among the internal circumstances was the national character of the inhabitants, who were known to be sturdier and straighter than those of other provinces, and were expected to present more fully a *tabula rasa*, for the proceedings of British rule. The Board had an insight into character, and a faculty for choosing men for the administration. Believing its own reputation, as well as the public good, to depend on this choice, it pursued the object with circumspection and single-mindedness. Though India is essentially the land of administrators, yet no governing body in any province has ever possessed at one time so many subordinates with talents applicable to so many branches, as the Board had for several years.

Thus the Board owed something to its auspicious star, but still more to its own innate power and inherent aptitude.

Apart from the general administration, some few measures may be noticed here as being peculiar to the Punjab. The first step after annexation was the disbandment of the late Sikh army. The men had been drawn chiefly from the class of peasant proprietors. They now reverted to the ancestral holdings, where their rights and interests were found to be secured by British arrangements. They were disarmed on being discharged, and no swords were left to be turned into ploughshares. But they settled down at once to agriculture, which was at that time more prosperous and profitable that it had ever been within living memory. Next, the people at large, by a disarming proclamation, were required to give up their arms. This they did without hesitation and almost without fail. Their minds had been overawed by the British victories and their spirit stupefied by recent defeat. This general disarming tended to the immediate pacification of the province, and ultimately proved of priceless advantage during the crisis which supervened eight years afterwards. If at that moment any men were disposed to raise their hands against us, they had no weapons to wield.

Then, defensive arrangements were made for the Trans-Indus Frontier, running as it did for full eight hundred miles at the base of the mountains which surround the valley of Peshawur and then stretching southwards, separate India from Afghanistan. The British border, thus formed, was itself inhabited by wild Moslem races, and was subject to incursions from still fiercer tribes dwelling in the adjacent hills. To guard this long-extended frontier a special body of troops, some twelve thousand men horse and foot, was organised and styled "The Punjab Frontier Force"; and it was placed not under the Commander-in-Chief of the Army, but under the Board of Administration. This frontier service immediately became an object of ambition to the European officers of the army as affording a school for soldiers and a field for distinction. Consequently the Board were able to draw from the ranks of the regular army many of the most promising officers of the day. The Native soldiers were recruited from among the most martial tribes in the border mountains, and the Native officers were chosen for personal merit and social status. Indeed this Force became perhaps the finest body of Native troops ever arrayed under British banners in India. As will be seen hereafter, it was able within eight years from this time to render signal service to the empire during the War of the Mutinies. In these arrangements the experience and talent of Henry Lawrence were conspicuously valuable.

Works of material improvement were at once to be undertaken in all parts of the province, and the Board were fortunate in being able to obtain for the direction of these operations the services of Major Robert Napier —now Lord Napier of Magdala.

In those days, before the introduction of railways,

the primary object was to construct the main trunk lines of roads. Such a trunk line had already been constructed through the older provinces from Calcutta to Delhi, a distance of about twelve hundred miles. The Board decided to continue this line from Delhi to Peshawur, a further distance of eight hundred miles. The viaducts over the Five Rivers were to be postponed, but the bridging of all lesser streams in the champaign country was to be undertaken, and especially a good passage made through the rugged region between the Jhelum and the Indus. At the outset, hopes were entertained that the Five Rivers would become the water-highways between this inland province and the coast, and be navigated by vessels with much steam power and yet with light draught. But there was difficulty for some years in building suitable vessels for service in the shifting and shallow channels; and in the end this idea vanished before the railway system which was advancing from the east.

In the land of the Five Rivers artificial irrigation occupied a prominent place. A new canal was now undertaken, to be drawn from the river Ravi, near the base of the Himalayas. It was to water the territory near Lahore the political capital, and Amritsar the religious centre, of the Sikhs. This territory was the home of the Sikh nationality and the most important part of the Punjab.

A feudal system had existed under the Sikh rule and ramified over the whole country. The status of the Native aristocracy depended mainly upon it. This system was absorbing much of the State resources, and could not be maintained under British rule. Its abolition gave rise to individual claims of intricacy, even of delicacy. These had to be treated generously and considerately so far as such treatment might consist with the policy itself, and with the just interests of public finance. In this department the kindly influence of Henry Lawrence was especially felt, and he did much to bridge over the gulf between Native and British rule.

In the civil administration the Board desired that, in the first instance at least, the forms of British procedure should be simplified, cheap speedy and substantial justice dispensed, and affairs conducted after what was termed the patriarchal model. The native races here were more frank in their utterance, more open in their demeanour, more direct in all their ways, than is usual in most parts of India. Every European officer was directed to cultivate from the outset a friendly understanding with them, so as to banish all sense of strangeness from their minds, and to make them feel at home and at ease under the British rule. This object is indeed aimed at universally in India, but it was attained with unrivalled success in the Punjab, and thereby was laid the foundation of that popular contentment which stood the Government in good stead during the season of dire trial eight years later in 1857.

The intense application, bestowed by the Board on many diverse subjects simultaneously, aggravated the toils of the members. But they derived relief and benefit from the division of labour (already mentioned) whereby for ordinary business the political and military branches were allotted to Henry, the fiscal and financial to John, the judicial to Montgomery.

In the fiscal department John found the noblest sphere for his special ability, because herein was included the settlement of the land revenue, the all-important scope of which has been explained in a preceding chapter. Then despite his unfavourable recollections of Etawah in 1838-39, he must have looked back with some gratitude to that place which had given him priceless experience in settlement-work. Here he was, happily for the Punjab, at home and in his element; as a consequence the field-survey, the assessment of the land-tax, the adjudication of rights and interests, the registration of tenures, were conducted with admirable completeness, promptitude and efficiency. He well knew that such operations were not likely to be turned out complete offhand; the affairs themselves were novel both to the officials and to the people; errors, failures, oversights, would occur, but he would have them rectified, again and again, until at last after re-constructing, re-casting, re-writing,—a full, accurate and abiding result was obtained. This cardinal operation has been one of the first cares of the Government in every province of India; but in no province has it ever been effected so completely, within a comparatively short time, as it was in the Punjab under his supervision. Its success conduced largely to that popular contentment which proved a bulwark of safety to British rule, during the danger which eight years afterwards menaced the Province.

Before the Native population, before the world, and for the most part before the European officers, the Board preserved an unbroken front and kept up the appearance of solidarity. But though the wheels of the great machine moved powerfully, and with apparent smoothness, still within the Board itself there was increasing friction. It became known, not perhaps to the public, but to the European officers around the centre of affairs, that Henry and John were not always in accord regarding policy and practice. And this matter affected the future for both of them, and especially for John.

Between Henry and John there was agreement in many essential matters such as the military occupation and the pacification of the province, the guarding of the Trans-Indus Frontier, the political relations with the Native States comprised within the Punjab, the development of material resources, the progressive policy of the administration. They were absolutely united in the diffusion of zeal among all grades and classes of officers and officials, and in stamping the best possible characteristics upon the public service. But they differed more or less on certain other points, and this difference must unavoidably be noticed, however briefly, because among other consequences, it had a considerable effect on the subsequent career of John. It was, however, official only and did not affect the sentiments of admiration and affection with which each regarded the other.

The difference then related to three points: the system of collecting the land revenue, the management of the finances, and the treatment of the feudal classes on the introduction of British rule. Some brief allusion must be made to each of these three points.

Under Native rule the land revenue had been collected sometimes in kind and sometimes in cash. John abhorred the system of collection in kind, as being the parent of oppressive abuses. His voice was consonant with the best traditions of British rule, and was at first popular with the agriculturists. But from various circumstances the prices of produce fell for several years abnormally, and the men had difficulty in obtaining money for their produce wherewith to pay their land-tax in cash. So they began to ask that it might as heretofore be paid in kind. Henry, partly from tenderness to old customs under Native rule, partly too from want of familiarity with fiscal abuses, inclined his ear to these murmurs which were indeed coming to be requests. John of course insisted on the cash system being maintained, though he was willing, indeed anxious, that the tax should be so assessed that the people could pay it easily even in the altered circumstances.

The finance of the province was ever present to the mind of John. Though keenly anxious for improvements of all sorts, he held that such measures must be regulated according to the financial means available within the province. Henry would not deny this in theory but would overlook it in practice. Having initiated projects tending to civilisation in a newly annexed province, he would press them forward without adequately considering how the cost was to be defrayed. He had an inner conviction that once a very desirable thing had been accomplished successfully, the difficulties on the score of expenses would either vanish or right themselves.

The treatment of the feudal classes on the introduction of British rule depended on a certain method which had been adopted under Native rule in the Punjab as in other parts of India. The land revenue belonged to and was the mainstay of the State. The ruler of the day would assign to an individual the revenue thus receivable from specified lands or villages. The right of the assignee extended only to the receipt of the land revenue. It did not necessarily affect the right to the property, that is to say, he had not thereby any title to collect the rent, as that would depend on whether he did or did not acquire the property. The assignment would be made generally on one or other of three grounds, the maintenance of religious establishments, the bestowal of favour, the reward or remuneration of services. The difference of opinion between Henry and John showed itself less on the first of the three grounds, but more on the second, and still further on the third. The discussion between the two brothers on the third or feudal ground may be summarised in this wise.

The Native ruler or sovereign would assign temporarily to his chieftains the land revenue of certain villages, or whole tracts of territory, on the condition of feudal service, chiefly military, being rendered. This service is not wanted under British rule, and cannot be maintained; then the question arises whether the assignment of the land revenue is to be continued. Similarly, allowances in cash from the State treasury are made to local chiefs in consideration of duty nominal or real being performed. This duty cannot be accepted under British rule, and a discussion springs up regarding the extent to which the allowances are to be withdrawn. When these cases exist on a large scale, involving extensive interests, it will be seen at a glance that there is much room for divergence of opinion between statesmen equally able, humane and conscientious. Henry thought that liberal concessions ought to be made to these feudal classes, for reasons of policy in allaying discontent among influential sections of the community. He held that the greater part of the former grants ought to be continued, although the obligation of service might be remitted. This must be effected, despite the financial cost which such arrangements might involve. John would rejoin that these grants must at once be curtailed, and provision made for their cessation on the demise of present incumbents. The government could not bear the double expense of continuing grants for the old service just dispensed with, and of defraying the charge of the newly organized service which the British Government must introduce according to its own ideas.

This is but a bare summary of a large and complex question, affecting not only thousands but tens of thousands of cases scattered all over the country. Upon such a question as this the social contentment and the financial equilibrium of the province largely depended. This much of notice is needed in order to show how the matter concerned the career and fortunes of John.

The Governor-General, Lord Dalhousie, became aware of the growing difference of opinion between Henry and John, but viewing it from afar he thought at first that more good than harm would result. He had the highest respect for both the brothers, but knowing them to have an independent will and potential force of character, he surmised that each might be inclining towards an extreme and that one would correct the other. Moreover he saw that the friction produced apparently that mental heat which supplied force to move the administration on and on towards success. With the excellent results displayed before him in the "First Punjab Report" in 1852, he was little disposed to interfere with the mechanism, and hoped that the two eminent brothers might gradually learn *componere lites.* But afterwards he began to perceive that this difference was working harm inasmuch as the discussions not only produced delay, but sometimes caused important matters to be put aside on account of the diversity of argument, for which no solution could be found.

Had these conditions lasted, moreover, an additional evil must have arisen ; for in the ranks of the public service two parties would have sprung up. Each brother was loyal to the other, and was as reticent as possible regarding the difference in opinion between them. Still inevitably the fact transpired, and accordingly some officers agreed with Henry and others with John. Though these good men obeyed orders, yet those orders would be issued only after their views had been submitted and considered. These views would become tinged with the colouring of the thought in two schools of opinion. It must be added that the Natives, who had concessions to ask, were persuasively insistent with their requests. Eloquence is one of nature's gifts to Oriental races. The skill with which a native will plead his cause in the ear of a listening official, is conceivable only to those Europeans who have experienced it. In these particular cases much that was dramatic or historical, affecting or pathetic, would be urged. Even the sterner mind of John would be touched sometimes, and much more so the more susceptible heart of Henry. Then the susceptibilities of the latter would be taken up by the officers who had been chosen by him for service in the Punjab. In the turn which events took, the formation of two parties, and the detriment to the public service which would have followed, were avoided.

Soon Lord Dalhousie and his Council at Calcutta concluded that an opportunity must be taken to effect a change; and that as one only of the two brothers should remain in the Punjab, John must be the man. While this conclusion was affecting the mind of the Governor-General, it so happened that, on an important vacancy occurring elsewhere, both brothers simultaneously offered to resign their positions in the Punjab and take service in some other part of India. This precipitated the decision of the Supreme Government.

That decision was communicated to Henry Lawrence by Lord Dalhousie in a memorable letter, from which some passages may be quoted to show historically how the matter stood.

"It has for some time been the recorded opinion of the Supreme Government that, whenever an opportunity occurred for effecting a change, the administration of the Punjab would best be conducted by a Chief Commissioner, having a Judicial and a Revenue Commissioner under him. But it was also the opinion of the Government that, whenever the change should be made, the Chief Commissioner ought to be an officer of the Civil Service. You stand far too high, and have received too many assurances and too many proofs of the great estimation in which your ability, qualities, and services have been held by the successive governments under which you have been employed, to render it necessary that I should bear testimony here to the value which has been set upon your labours and upon your service as the head of the administration of the Punjab by the Government over which I have had the honour to preside. We do not regard it as in any degree disparaging to you that we, nevertheless, do not consider it expedient to commit the sole executive charge of the administration of a kingdom to any other than to a thoroughly trained and experienced civil officer. Although the Regulations do not prevail in the Punjab, and although the system of civil government has wisely and successfully been made more simple in its forms, still we are of opinion that the superintendence of so large a system, everywhere founded on the Regulations, and pervaded by their spirit, can be thoroughly controlled and moulded, as changes from time to time may become necessary, only by a civilian fully versed in the system of the elder provinces and experienced in its operation.

"As the Government entertained these views, it became evident that the change it contemplates in the form of administration could not be effected, nor could the dissensions existing be reconciled, unless it were agreeable to you to transfer your services to some other department.

"The result of our consideration was the statement I have now to make, that if you are willing to accept Rajputana, the Government will be happy to appoint you to it, with a view to effecting the change of the form of administration in the Punjab, to which I have already referred."

So Henry departed for Rajputana in 1853, with honour acknowledged of all men, and amidst the sorrowing farewells of friends, European and Native. He left a fragrant memory behind him as he crossed the Sutlej for the last time on his way to Rajputana, whither countless good wishes followed his course. But no man then anticipated the grave events which, within four years, would open out for him in Oude a sphere as grand as that which he was now quitting.

Thus after a term of four years' service in the Board of Administration, that is from 1849 to 1853, John Lawrence was left in sole command of the Punjab. But though his nerve was unimpaired, his capacity developed, his experience enlarged, he was not physically the same man at the end of this term that he was at the beginning. In October, 1850, at Lahore, he had been stricken down by a severe fever, as bad as that from which he had suffered just ten years previously at Etawah, and his health never was fully restored after that shock. He, however, recovered sufficiently to accompany Lord Dalhousie on a march in the Punjab during the winter months, and afterwards in the following spring 1851 to examine the condition of the Peshawur valley. The ensuing months he spent at Simla in company with his wife and children.

Then, for the first time in his toil-worn life, he enjoyed the blessings of a Himalayan retreat, after the torrid heat and the depressing damp of twenty previous summers. He resorted thither, not on leave but on duty, by the special direction of Lord Dalhousie who was there also. He was indeed obliged to quit Lahore for that summer, and had not a retreat to Simla been open to him, he must for a time have relinquished his office in the Punjab. As he ascended the Simla mountains, seven to nine thousand feet above sea-level, the sight of the Himalayas was not new to him, for he had seen them in the Trans-Sutlej States; twice also he had paid brief visits to Simla itself. How pleasant, then, through the summer of 1851, was it for him to bask in mild sunshine, to drink in the balmy air, to recline in the shadows of oaken glades, to roam amidst forests of pine and cedar, to watch the light gilding peak after peak in the snowy range at sunrise, to perceive through a field-glass at sunset the familiar Sutlej winding like the thinnest of silver threads through the distant plains, to note the rain-clouds rolling up the mountain sides, to hear the thunder-peals echo among the crags! These things would have been delights to him even as a visitor in the easiest circumstances, in hale robustness, in all the pride of life; but no pen can describe what they were to the over-taxed brain, the strained nerves, the fevered constitution, the shaken strength—such as his. He revived apace and remained in official harness, having taken the most important part of his work with him, and receiving by the daily post his papers and despatches from Lahore. Further, he had the advantage of personal intercourse with Lord Dalhousie, and thus formed a friendship which, at first official, soon became personal. After two or three months of this changed life, his old vivacity returned, and his conversation was almost as it had been in England and Ireland. But recurrence of Indian fever after an interval is almost a rule, and his case was no exception. At Simla in the autumn his Lahore fever reappeared severely, just a year after its original appearance. This time he was stronger to meet the attack, and so threw it off. But he rose from the sick-bed, for the second time in thirteen months, with vitality impaired. He was, as the event proved, sufficiently recovered to escape any serious illness for nearly three years, and to work without interruption till 1854. But during this summer of 1851, he calmly reviewed his position. He thus actually prepared himself for closing the important part of his career, and for speedily retiring from the public service. With his usual forethought, and in his unassuming way, he would reckon up his resources, and estimate how to live in some quiet and inexpensive place in England on a modest competency. But Providence decreed otherwise, and the possible necessity, though ever borne in mind, did not reach the point of action. So in the early winter he returned to his post at Lahore, to mix in all the troublous discussions, and to bear the official fatigues which have been already mentioned, until the spring of 1853, from which point our narrative takes a fresh departure.

Though now left, in his own phrase, to walk alone—the very course most acceptable to him—he ever remembered his absent brother. In after years he was anxious that Henry's name should be linked with his own in the annals of the Punjab. At Lahore in 1864, at the culminating point of his fame, and in the plenitude of his authority—when the memory of former differences had long been buried in his brother's grave—he used these words in a speech to the assembled princes and chiefs of the province: "My brother Henry and I governed this province. You all knew him well, and his memory will ever dwell in your hearts as a ruler who was a real friend of the people. We studied to make ourselves acquainted with the usages, feelings and wants of every class and race, and to improve the condition of all."

CHAPTER VI

CHIEF COMMISSIONER OF THE PUNJAB

1853-1857

THE governing idea, as set forth at the outset of the last chapter, must be sustained in this chapter also. The administration of the Punjab, already sketched, must be yet further delineated; for upon its completeness depended the ability and sufficiency of the province to keep its own head aloft in the rising tide, and to hold up its neighbours amidst the dashing breakers of the rebellion destined to occur only four years later. We need not ask what would have happened had the Punjab been governed with feebleness and inefficiency, because such defects are not to be anticipated under British rule; but the chance was this, that even under an ordinarily fair administration, the preparation of the province might not have been effected within the too short time allowed by events,—that, for instance, the pacification had not been perfect, the frontier tribes not entirely over-awed, the dangerous classes not fully disarmed, the feudal classes not conciliated by timely concessions, the land-settlement not complete, the agrarian disputes not quite composed, the official establishments not so organized as to call forth all the provincial resources at a moment's notice. For all these things in combination, an extraordinarily good administration was needed, and that the Punjab had. Without that, the province must have been submerged by the floods of rebellion in 1857, and then all Northern India, the finest part of the Indian empire, must have succumbed.

John Lawrence was now, during the spring of 1853, installed in the sole and chief command of the Punjab, with the title of Chief Commissioner, and without any colleague of equal station with himself. This title was created on this occasion for the first time in India, and has since been borne by other men in other provinces; but the fact of its being originally borne by him has invested it with peculiar dignity, and rendered every one proud to bear it. The Punjab had been divided from the beginning of British rule, under his Board, into seven divisions, each being under the civil command of a Commissioner—namely, the Cis-Sutlej on the east of that river, the Trans-Sutlej on the west, the central or Lahore division round the capital, the southern division around Mooltan near the confluence of the Indus and its tributaries, the Sind Sagar division on the east of the Middle Indus,—Sind being the original name of Indus—the Peshawur division comprising that famous valley with the surrounding hills, and the Derajat division at the base of the Sulemani range dividing India from Afghanistan. These seven divisions or commissionerships being placed under him, he was styled the Chief Commissioner. In the management of the country he was assisted by two high officers styled the Judicial Commissioner for law and justice, and the Financial Commissioner for revenue and general administration. His colleague in the late Board, Montgomery, filled the Judicial Commissionership. The Financial Commissionership was, after a year, filled by Donald Macleod, who had been for some time Commissioner of the Trans-Sutlej division. Macleod was eminently worthy of this post in all respects save one. Though prompt and attentive in ordinary affairs, and most useful in emergencies, he had a habit of procrastination in matters requiring deliberative thought. Despite this drawback, he was one of the most eminent men then in India. His scholar-like acquirements, his profound knowledge of eastern life and manners, his refined intellect and polished manner, rendered him an ornament to the Punjab service. Moreover, he had a serene courage, a calm judgment amidst turmoil and peril, which, during the troublous years to come, stood him and his country in good stead.

Thus John Lawrence was blessed with two coadjutors after his own heart, who were personally his devoted friends, who set before all men the example which he most approved, and diffused around the very tone which he wished to prevail. He was in complete accord with them; they were proud to support him, he was thankful to lean on them. No doubt the recent tension with his brother, amidst the urgency of affairs, had affected his health. With him as with other men, the anxiety of undecided controversy, the trial of the temper, the irritating annoyance of reiterated argument, caused more wear and tear than did labour and responsibility. But now he began to have halcyon days officially. His spirits rose as the fresh air of undivided responsibility braced his nerves. Though far from being physically the man he was before the illness of 1850, he was yet sufficiently well to give a full impulse to the country and its affairs, and he girded himself with gladness for the work before him. Like the good ship *Argo* of old, he propelled himself with his own native force—

> "Soon as clear'd the harbour—like a bird—
> *Argo* sprang forward with a bound, and bent
> Her course across the water-path."

The administration of the county proceeded in the same course, even along the same lines and in the same grooves, under him as under the late Board. There may have been some change in tendency here and there, or rather existing tendencies may have been drawn a little in this or that direction; but for the most part he introduced no perceptible modification. This fact may appear strange, when the differences of opinion between him and his brother are remembered. These differences, however, had been reserved as much as possible for discussion *inter se*, and so kept back from the public eye; thus many important matters had for a time been laid aside; consequently he had not anything to undo in these matters, for in fact nothing had finally been done. So he had no decisions to reverse in cases which had for a while been left undecided. But being relieved from the irritation of controversy, he paid more regard to the known opinions or the recorded convictions of his now absent brother, than perhaps he had done when the brother was present to press the counter-arguments. Thus he succeeded in carrying on the administration without any external break of continuity. If anything like the formation or growth of two schools or parties of opinion among the civil officers had begun, that ceased and disappeared at once. All men knew that the public policy would be directed by one guiding hand, and that when all those who had a claim to be consulted had said their say, a decision would be pronounced which must be obeyed *ex animo.* But this obedience was rendered easy, because no marked deflection from former principle or procedure was perceptible. It had for some time been notified in various ways that the expenses were growing too fast for the income, and greater financial strictness would be required. None were surprised, therefore, when a more rigid adjustment of expenditure in reference to revenue, and of outlay to resources, was introduced. The Board had designed to adjust the income and expenses so that the Province should from its provincial revenues defray the cost of its administration and contribute a share towards defraying the cost of the army cantoned within its limits; and he carried that financial design into full effect. It was not expected of him that his Province should pay for the whole of that army which defended the empire as well as the Province. But he managed that his provincial treasury should give its proper quota.

In most, perhaps almost all, other respects the conduct of business was the same as that described as existing under the late Board. The march of affairs was rapid and the stream flowed smoothly. The only novelty would be the introduction of additional improvements according to the opportunities of each succeeding year, and the growing requirements of the time. Such improvements were a brief digest of Native law and of British procedure for the use of the courts of justice, commonly called at the time the Punjab Code; the taking of a census and other statistics; the introduction of primary education under State agency, and others.

In weighing the burden which now fell on John Lawrence's shoulders, it is to be remembered that though before the public and at the bar of history he was the virtual Governor of the Punjab, yet the Government was not technically vested in him, nor had he the status and title of Lieutenant-Governor. As Chief Commissioner he was the deputy of, or the principal executive authority under, the Governor-General in Council. Not only was he under the constant control of the Government of India, but also he had to obtain the specific sanction of that supreme authority for every considerable proceeding, and for the appointment of every man to any office of importance. Being high in the confidence of the Government of India, he was almost always able to obtain the requisite sanction, which was, as a general rule, given considerately and generously. On a historic retrospect it may appear that he ought then to have been appointed Lieutenant-Governor of the Punjab, on an equal footing with the Lieutenant-Governors of the North-Western Provinces and of Bengal, and that he who really did the work and bore the responsibility should also have had the rank and the status. But at that time *dîs aliter visum.* The point ought however to be mentioned here, because it greatly affected the extent of his labours and anxieties. It was one thing for him to devise and arrange what ought to be done, and to prepare for carrying it out; but it was an additional thing for him to obtain the sanction on grounds to be set forth in every important case. The selection of the right men to fill the various offices of trust fell upon him. But instead of appointing them straightway to the places, he had to obtain sanction, in view of which sanction some explanation would have to be rendered. Sometimes, too, the Government of India might desire to appoint some officer other than the one whom he had recommended. Thereupon he would be sure to press his view, believing that the success and efficiency of his work depended on the fitting man being placed in the right position. Being regarded by the Governor-General with generous confidence, he almost invariably carried his point. But the correspondence, official and private, caused hereby was considerable, and the anxiety was greater still. But although as Chief Commissioner he found the work more laborious than it would have been to him as Lieutenant-Governor, still he gladly accepted the position with this drawback, because within his jurisdiction he had his own way. He must come to an understanding with the Government of India indeed; but once he had succeeded in that, no colleague at home, no high officer near his provincial throne, could challenge his policy. This autonomy, even with its unavoidable limitations, was a great boon to a man of his temperament.

Having set to work under new and favourable conditions, he pursued his task with what in many men would be termed ardour and enthusiasm. These qualities were evinced by him, no doubt, but in his nature they were over-borne by persistency and determination. Thus it would be more correct to say that he urged on the chariot of state with disciplined energy. He well knew, as the Board before him had known, that the results of large operations must in the long run be well reported for public information. But he held that the reporting might be deferred for a short season. Meanwhile he would secure actual success; the work should from beginning to end be accurately tested; it should be tempered and polished like steel and finished *usque ad unguem.* Some officers would ensure an excellent quality of work with great pains, but then they would fall short in quantity; others would despatch a vast quantity, but then it would be of inferior quality; he would have both quality and quantity, all the work that came to hand must be performed in time, but then it must also be done well. Nothing is more common even for able administrators than to lean too much towards one or the other of these two alternatives; no man ever held the balance between the two better than he, and very few could hold it as well. In no respect was his pre-eminence as an administrator more marked than in this. In the first instance he would prepare no elaborate despatches, indite no minutes, order no detailed reports to be prepared, write no long letters. He would have action absolutely, and work rendered complete. His management of men may be aptly described by the following lines from Coleridge's translation of Schiller:

"Well for the whole, if there be found a man
Who makes himself what nature destined him,
The pause, the central point, to thousand thousands—
Stands fixed and stately like a firm-built column.

. . . . .

"How he incites and strengthens all around him,
Infusing life and vigour. Every power
Seems as it were redoubled by his presence;
He draws forth every latent energy,
Showing to each his own peculiar talent."

He knew that an administrator shines, not only in what he does himself, but also in what he induces others to do, that his policy will in part be tested by the character of the men whom he raises up around him, that the master is recognised in his pupils, and that if his work is to live after him, he must have those ready who will hand on the tradition, and will even take his place should he fall in the battle of life. His aim, then, was to establish a system and found a school.

During 1853 and the early part of 1854 he remained in fair health, though not in full strength according to his normal standard. During the early summer of 1854 he sojourned at Murri, a Himalayan sanatorium in the region between the Jhelum and the Indus. At this sanatorium, six to eight thousand feet above sea-level, he enjoyed the advantages which have been already described in reference to Simla. His horizon was bounded by the snowy ranges that overlook the valley of Cashmere. About midsummer he returned to his head-quarters at Lahore in the hottest time of the year, and he was once more stricken down with illness, from the effects of which he certainly did not recover during the remainder of his career in the Punjab. Fever there was with acute nervous distress, but it was in the head that the symptoms were agonizing. He said with gasps that he felt as if *rakshas* (Hindoo mythological giants) were driving prongs through his brain. The physicians afforded relief by casting cold douches of water on his head; but when the anguish was over his nerve-system seemed momentarily injured. Afterwards when alluding to attacks of illness, he would say that he had once or twice been on the point of death. Perhaps this may have been one of the occasions in his mind. For a man of his strength the attack hardly involved mortal danger; still it was very grave and caused ill effects to ensue. After a few days he rallied rapidly, went back to Murri, and resumed his work, disposing of the arrears which in the interval had accumulated. Doubtless he returned to duty too soon for his proper recovery, but this was unavoidable.

After 1854 he spent the summer months of each year at Murri, having been urged to do so by the Governor-General, Lord Dalhousie.

At various times he visited several of the Native States under his charge, exchanging courtesies, conforming to their ceremonial usages, holding Oriental levees, and mixing in scenes of Asiatic pomp amidst localities of exceeding picturesqueness. He strove to set the seal on their contentment—hardly anticipating how soon he would have to require them to draw their swords for the Empire. He again visited Peshawur, directed operations against some offending hill-tribes, and marched along the whole Trans-Indus frontier.

In 1854 he caused a report of his civil administration to be prepared. This report recounted the efforts made for imparting force and vigour to the police, simplicity and cheapness to civil justice, popularity to municipal institutions, salubrity and discipline to the prisons, security to the landed tenures, moderation as well as fixity to the land-tax. It narrated the beginning of a national education, and the establishment of institutions such as dispensaries and hospitals, evincing a practical interest in the well-being of the people. It adverted specially to the construction of roads and bridges in the face of physical difficulties, the excavation of canals, the patrolling of the highways and the erection of caravan-serais. None could then foresee the enormous service which these highways would render to the British cause during the troubles which were in store for the country.

In corroboration of this summary, the following testimony was afterwards afforded in 1859 in a farewell address presented to him by his officers, when he was about to lay down his power, and to quit them perhaps for ever. Most of them were either eye-witnesses, or otherwise personally cognisant, of what they relate.

"Those among us who have served in political and diplomatic capacities know how you have preserved friendly relations, during critical and uncertain times, with the native principalities by which this province is surrounded; how, all along an extended, rugged, and difficult frontier, you have successfully maintained an attitude of consistency and resolution with wild and martial tribes, neither interfering unduly, on the one hand, nor yielding anything important on the other.

"Those among us who are immediately connected with the civil administration know how, in the interior of the country, you have kept the native chiefs and gentry truc to their allegiance by strictness tempered with conciliation; how emphatically you have been the friend of the middle and lower classes among the natives, the husbandman, the artisan, and the labourer. They know how, with a large measure of success, you have endeavoured to moderate taxation; to introduce judicial reforms; to produce a real security of life and property; to administer the finances in a prudent and economical spirit; to further the cause of material improvements, advancing public works so far as the means, financial and executive, of the Government might permit; to found a popular system of secular education; to advocate the display of true Christianity before the people, without infringing those principles of religious toleration which guide the British Government in dealing with its native subjects. They know how you have always administered patronage truly and indifferently for the good of the State. To the civil officers you have always set the best example and given the soundest precepts, and there are many who are proud to think that they belong to your school."

In this address the maintenance of order along the frontier Trans-Indus is mentioned prominently, and indeed this thorny subject had engaged his attention almost incessantly. He had been obliged frequently to order military expeditions against the martial and intractable tribes inhabiting that wild border. No such difficult frontier having previously been incorporated in British India, his policy though unavoidable was in some degree novel, and the public mind became at times agitated, perhaps even mistrustful of the necessity for this frequent recourse to arms. In 1855, at Lord Dalhousie's suggestion, he caused his Secretary to draw up a report of the expeditions which had been undertaken, and of the offences which had afforded not only justification but grounds of necessity. That report was an exposition of his frontier policy at the time.

This frontier was described as being eight hundred miles in length. The tribes were grouped in two categories, one having one hundred and thirty-five thousand, the other eighty thousand fighting men, real warriors, brave and hardy, well armed though undisciplined. After a precise summary of the chronic and heinous offences perpetrated by each tribe within British territory, the character of the tribes generally was set forth. They were savages, noble savages perhaps, and not without some tincture of generosity. They had nominally a religion, but Mahommedanism, as understood by them, was no better, or perhaps actually worse, than the creeds of the wildest races on earth. In their eyes the one great commandment was blood for blood. They were never without weapons: when grazing their cattle, when driving beasts of burden, when tilling the soil, they bore arms. Every tribe and section of a tribe had its internecine wars, every family its hereditary blood-feuds, and every individual his personal foes. Each tribe had a debtor and creditor account with its neighbours, life for life.

They had descended from the hills and fought their battles out in our territory; they had plundered or burnt our villages and slain our subjects; they had for ages regarded the plain as their preserve, and its inhabitants as their game. When inclined for cruel sport, they had sallied forth to rob and murder, and occasionally took prisoners into captivity for ransom. They had fired upon our troops, and even killed our officers in our own territories. They traversed at will our territories, entered our villages, traded in our markets; but few British subjects, and no servant of the British Government, would dare to enter their country on any account whatever.

On the other hand the British Government had recognised their independence; had confirmed whatever fiefs they held within its territory; had never extended its jurisdiction one yard beyond the old limits of the Sikh dominions or of the Punjab as we found it. It had abstained from any interference in, or connection with, their affairs. Though permitting and encouraging its subjects to defend themselves at the time of attack, it had prevented them from retaliating afterwards and making reprisals. Though granting refuge to men flying for their lives, it had never allowed armed bodies to seek protection in its territory. It had freely permitted these independent hill-people to settle, to cultivate, to graze their herds, and to trade in its territories. It had accorded to such the same protection, rights, privileges, and conditions as to its own subjects. It had freely admitted them to its hospitals and dispensaries; its medical officers had tended scores of them in sickness, and sent them back to their mountain homes cured. The ranks of its service were open to them, so that they might eat our salt and draw our pay if so inclined.

Then a list was given of the expeditions, some fifteen in number, against various tribes between 1849 and 1855, and the policy of these expeditions was declared to be reasonable and just. If murder and robbery still went on, in spite of patience, of abstinence from provocation and of conciliation, then what but force remained? Was the loss of life and property with the consequent demoralisation to continue or to be stopped? If it could only be stopped by force, then was not force to be applied? The exertion of such force had proved to be successful. The tribes after chastisement usually professed and evinced repentance. They entered into engagements, and for the first time began to keep their faith. They never repeated the offences which had brought on the punishment. In almost every case an aggressive tribe behaved badly before, and well after, suffering from an expedition.

By this policy the foundation was laid of a pacification whereby these border tribes were kept quiet most fortunately during the trouble of 1857, which is soon to be narrated. Had a feeble or inefficient treatment been adopted towards them from the beginning, they would have become thereby emboldened to rush upon us in the hour of our weakness. As it was, they had been accustomed to a firm yet just policy. The awe of us still rested on them for a while, and they refrained from mischief at a time when they might have done grievous damage. Further, this policy, steadily promoted by Lawrence's successors for fully twenty years, has rendered the British border Trans-Indus one of the most satisfactory portions of the Indian empire. In no line of country is the difference between British and Oriental rule more conspicuous than in this.

The consideration of the Frontier Policy, up to the end of 1856, leads up to the relations between Afghanistan and India. The Punjab as the adjoining province became naturally the medium of such relations.

Up to 1854 the administrators of the Punjab had no concern in the affairs of Afghanistan. The Amir, Dost Mahommed, who had been reinstated after the first Afghan war, in 1843, was still on the throne, but he was far advanced in years, and dynastic troubles were expected on his death. Since the annexation of the Punjab, he and his had given no trouble whatever to the British. The intermittent trouble, already mentioned on the Trans-Indus Frontier, arose not from the Afghans proper, but from border tribes who were practically independent of any government in Afghanistan. But by the events connected with the Crimean war in 1854, British apprehensions, which had been quiescent for a while, were again aroused in reference to Central Asia generally, and to Afghanistan as our nearest neighbour.

The idea, which has in later years assumed a more distinct form, then arose that Russia would make diversions in Central Asia in order to counteract any measures which England might adopt towards Turkey. This caused John Lawrence to express for the first time his official opinion on the subject. He would, if possible, have nothing to do with Afghanistan. If Russia were to advance as an enemy towards India, he would not meet her by way of Afghanistan. He would await such advance upon the Indus frontier, which should be rendered for her impassable. The counteracting movement by England should, in his opinion, be made not in Asia but in Europe; and Russia should be so attacked in the Baltic and the Black Sea, that she would be thereby compelled to desist from any attempt to harass India from the quarter of Central Asia.

In these days he received a deputation from the Khan of Kokand, one of the three well-known Khanates adjoining Siberia, who feared absorption into the Russian empire. But he deemed assistance from the British side to be impracticable, and after obtaining the instructions of Lord Dalhousie, he entertained the deputation kindly but sent it back with a negative reply; and the Khan's fear of absorption was soon afterwards realised.

Then, in consequence of the hostile movements of Persia against Afghanistan, presumably with indirect support from Russia, he received proposals from Colonel (afterwards Sir Herbert) Edwardes, the talented and distinguished Commissioner of Peshawur, for an alliance with the Afghan ruler. He strongly advised the Governor-General not to enter into any relations with Afghanistan, but added, as in duty bound, that if such relations were to be undertaken, he would do his best to arrange them satisfactorily. He then, under Lord Dalhousie's direction, in company with Edwardes, met Sirdar Gholam Hyder the heir-apparent of the Amir Dost Mahommed at Peshawur in the spring of 1855. Thereupon he concluded a treaty, obliging the two parties mutually to respect each other's dominions, also binding the Amir to be the friend of the friends and the enemy of the enemies of the British Government, without imposing on it any corresponding obligation. But though the treaty was simple, his negotiations with the Afghan prince were complex, and in these he was duly assisted by Edwardes, with whom the policy had originated, and to whom he rendered full acknowledgment.

He was recommended by Lord Dalhousie for honours from the Crown, and was made a Knight Commander of the Bath early in 1856, just after Lord Dalhousie had been succeeded by Lord Canning.

He was shortly afterwards, in 1856, consulted by Lord Canning regarding the war which the British Government was declaring against Persia for her conduct towards Herat, a place then deemed to be the key of Afghanistan on the western side. In the autumn of that year he was startled by news of the fall of Herat into Persian hands, and by proposals from Edwardes for rendering effective aid to the Afghan Amir. Again he opposed these proposals, with an intimation that if the Governor-General, Lord Canning, should accept them he would do his utmost to secure their success. As they were accepted by the Government of India he repaired early in 1857 to Peshawur to meet the Amir

Dost Mahommed. At the Amir's special request, he crossed the British portal of the Khyber Pass, and proceeded for a full march inside that famous defile. The crags and heights echoed with the boom of the guns fired from the Afghan camp to salute his arrival. There was much of weirdness and wildness in the aspect of the Afghan levee which was there held in his honour, an aspect which betokened the desperate character of many of the chiefs there assembled. He was then accompanied by Dost Mahommed to Peshawur, and again assisted by Edwardes in the tedious negotiations which followed. He concluded an additional treaty with Dost Mahommed, confirming that which had been already made with Gholam Hyder, and agreeing to afford the Amir a subsidy of a lac of rupees, or £10,000, monthly with a present of four thousand stand of arms, on the condition that a European officer should be temporarily deputed, not to Caubul but to Candahar, and with an assurance that in deference to Afghan susceptibility, the British Government would not propose to despatch any European officer to Caubul unless circumstances should change.

This treaty established relations between the British empire and Afghanistan which have lasted, with some brief but stormy interruptions, for thirty years up to the present time. It was concluded on the eve of the war of those mutinies in India which were foreseen by neither of the contracting parties. On its conclusion Dost Mahommed exclaimed that he had thereby made with the British Government an alliance which he would keep till death; and he did keep it accordingly. As a consequence, during the storm, which very soon afterwards burst over Northern India up to the very verge of Afghanistan, he preserved a friendly neutrality which was of real value to the British cause. Thus whatever may be the arguments before or since that date, the beginning of 1857, for or against the setting up of relations with Afghanistan, this treaty proved very useful to British interests in the events which arose immediately after it was made.

It is but just to the memory of Edwardes, who was the originator and the prime adviser of this policy, to quote the explanation of it in his own words by a memorandum which he wrote in the following year, 1858. After alluding to the former dealings of the British with Afghanistan, he writes thus regarding himself:

"When Commissioner of Peshâwur, in 1854, he sought and obtained the permission of Lord Dalhousie to bring about that hearty reconciliation which was expressed in the first friendly treaty of March 1855, and subsequently (with the equally cordial approval of Lord Canning) was substantially consolidated by the treaty of January 26, 1857. At this latter juncture the Shah of Persia had seized Herat and was threatening Candahar. England was herself attacking Persia in the Gulf, and the Indian Government now gave to the Amir at Cabul eight thousand stand of arms, and a subsidy of £10,000 a month, so long as the Persian war should last. We did this, as the treaty truly said, 'out of friendship.' We did it, too, in the plenitude of our power and highnoon of that treacherous security which smiled on India in January 1857. How little, as we set our seals to that treaty, did we know that in May the English in India, from Peshâwur to the sea, would be fighting for empire and their lives, and that God's mercy was stopping the mouths of lions against our hour of need. To the honour of Dost Mahommed Khan let it be recorded that during the Sepoy war, under the greatest temptation from events and the constant taunts of the fanatical priests of Cabul, he remained true to the treaty, and abstained from raising the green flag of Islam and marching down on the Punjab."

In another memorandum discussing the alternatives, of advancing into Afghanistan to meet Russia, or of awaiting her attack on our own frontier—which frontier has just been described—and deciding in favour of the latter, Edwardes writes thus :

"By waiting on our present frontier, we husband our money, organise our line of defence, rest upon our base and railroads, save our troops from fatigue, and bring our heaviest artillery into the field ; while the enemy can only bring light guns over the passes, has to bribe and fight his way across Afghanistan, wears out and decimates his army, exhausts his treasure and carriage, and, when defeated, has to retreat through the passes and over all Afghanistan—plundered at every march by the tribes."

Early in 1857 all people in the Punjab, with John the Chief Commissioner at their head, rejoiced to hear that Henry Lawrence had been appointed by Lord Canning to be Chief Commissioner of Oude and would now occupy a position peculiarly suited to his genius.

The narrative, having now reached the month of April, 1857, may pause for a moment on the eve of a perilous crisis. In the coming events the Punjab was destined to play a foremost part, to be the staff for sustaining the empire and the sword for destroying its enemies. It may be well to review in the briefest terms the position which was about to undergo the severest test.

The Punjab had a considerable portion of the European army of India cantoned within its limits, and relatively to its size a larger proportion of European troops than any other province in the empire. Within its area every political centre, but not every strategic point, was held by European soldiers. The long extended frontier was quiet for a time at least, some evil-disposed tribes having been overawed and others deterred by punishment from transgressing. The Frontier Native Force was in efficient discipline and in high spirits; it had neither connection nor sympathy with the regular Sepoy army. The Himalayan State of Jammu-Cashmere, on the northern boundary, was loyal from gratitude for substantial benefits conferred. The lesser Native States in the country between the Jumna and the Sutlej were faithful in remembrance of protection accorded during full fifty years. Of the Native aristocracy, that portion which had a real root in the soil was flourishing fairly well, that which had not was withering away. With the feudal classes judicious concessions in land and money, not over-burdensome to the Treasury, had extinguished discontent which might otherwise have smouldered till it burst into a flame if fanned by the gale which was soon to blow over the province. The middle classes living on the land, the yeomen, the peasant proprietors, the village communities, all felt a security never known before. Favourable seasons had caused abundant harvests, and the agricultural population was prospering. The military classes of the Sikh nationality had settled down to rural industry. The land-settlement had provided livelihood and occupation for all the men of thews and sinews, who formed the flower of the population or the nucleus of possible armies, and who really possessed the physical force of the country. The fighting men, interspersed amidst the civil population, had given up their arms to the authorities. In the British metaphor of the time, the teeth of the evil-disposed had been completely drawn. Trade had developed under the new rule, and had expanded with improved means of communication. Capital had begun to accumulate, and the moneyed classes were in favour of a government that would support public credit and refrain from extortion. The mass of the people were contented, prices being cheap, wages on the rise and employment brisk. The provincial revenues were elastic and increasing, though the assessments were easier, the taxation lighter, and the imposts fewer than formerly. The transit-dues, erst vexatiously levied under Native rule, had been abolished. The whole administration had been so framed as to ensure a strong though friendly grasp of the province, its people, its resources, its capabilities. The bonds were indeed to be worn easily, but they had been cast in a vast fold all round the country and could be drawn tighter at pleasure. The awe inspired by British victories still dwelt in the popular mind. As the repute of the late Sikh army had been great, that of their conquerors became greater still. The people were slow to understand the possibility of disaster befalling so puissant a sovereignty as that which had been set up before their eyes. The system was being administered by a body of European officers, trained in the highest degree for organised action and for keeping a tenacious grip upon their districts. Every post of importance was filled by a capable man, many posts by men of talent, and some even by men of genius. At the head of them all was John Lawrence himself, whose eye penetrated to every compartment of the State-ship to prove and test her as seaworthy.

Notes of warning had been sounded from Umballa, the military station midway between the Jumna and the Sutlej. Beyond the Sutlej in the Punjab proper no unfavourable symptom was perceptible. But day by day ominous sounds seemed to be borne northwards in the very air. At first they were like the mutterings of a far off thunderstorm. Then they were as the gathering of many waters. Soon they began to strike the ear of the Punjab administrator, who might say as the anxious settler in North America said,

> "Hark ! 'tis the roll of the Indian drum."

CHAPTER VII

WAR OF THE MUTINIES

1857-1859

THE story has now arrived at the month of May, 1857, and its hero is about "to take up arms against a sea of troubles." It may be well, then, to remember what his position was according to the Constitution of British India.

Of all lands, British India is the land of discipline in the best sense of the term, and its component parts, though full of self-help and individuality, are blended into one whole by subordination to a supreme authority. If in times of trouble or danger every proconsul or prefect were to do what is best in his own eyes for his territory without due regard to the central control, then the British Indian empire would soon be as other Asiatic empires have been. A really great Anglo-Indian must be able to command within the limits of his right, and to obey loyally where obedience is due from him. But if he is to expect good instructions from superior authority, then that authority must be well informed. Therefore he must be apt in supplying not only facts, but also suggestions as the issue of original and independent thought. He must also be skilled in cooperating with those over whom he has no actual authority, but whose assistance is nevertheless needed. In dangerous emergency he must do his utmost if instructions from superior authority cannot be had in time. But he must take the line which such authority, if consulted, would probably approve; and he must not prolong his separate action beyond the limit of real necessity. Often men, eminent on the whole, have been found to fail in one or other of these respects, and such failure has detracted from their greatness. John Lawrence was good in all these cardinal points equally; he could command, obey, suggest, co-operate, according to just requirements; therefore he was great all round as an administrator,—

> "Strong with the strength of the race
> To command, to obey, to endure."

When the Sepoy mutinies burst over Northern India, he was not the Governor of the Punjab, for the Government of that province was administered by the Governor-General in Council at Calcutta. Vast as was his influence, still he was only Chief Commissioner or chief executive authority in all departments, and Agent to the Governor-General. Subject to the same control, he had under his general command and at his disposal the Frontier Force described in the last chapter, an important body indeed but limited in numbers. In the stations and cantonments of the regular army, European and Native, he had the control of the barracks, the buildings and all public works. But with the troops he had nothing to do, and over their commanders he had no authority.

After the interruption of communication between the Punjab and Calcutta on the outbreak of the Mutinies, his position was altered by the force of events. Additional powers had not been delegated to him, indeed, by the Governor-General, but he was obliged to assume them in the series of emergencies which arose. He had to incur on his responsibility a vast outlay of money, and even to raise loans financially on the credit of the British Government, to enrol large bodies of Native soldiers, and appoint European officers from the regular troops to command them; to create, and allot salaries temporarily to, many new appointments—all which things lawfully required the authority of the Governor-General in Council, to whom, however, a reference was impossible during the disturbance. Again, he was obliged to make suggestions to the commanders of the regular troops at the various stations throughout the Province. These suggestions were usually accepted by them, and so had full effect. The commanders saw no alternative but to defer to him as he was the chief provincial authority, and as they were unable to refer to the Commander-in-Chief or to the Supreme Government. They also felt their normal obligation always to afford aid to him as representing the civil power in moments of need. Thus upon him was cast by rapid degrees the direction of all the British resources, civil, military and political, within the Punjab and its dependencies.

This explanation is necessary, in order to illustrate the arduous part which he was compelled to take in the events about to be noticed. Thus can we gauge his responsibility for that ultimate result, which might be either the steadfast retention of a conquest won eight years previously, or a desolating disaster. From such a far-inland position the Europeans might, he knew, be driven towards their ships at the mouth of the Indus, but how many would ever reach the haven must be terribly doubtful. There he stood, then, at the head of affairs, like a tower raised aloft in the Land of the Five Rivers, with its basis tried by much concussion, but never shaken actually. He had, as shown in the last chapter, resources unequalled in any province of India. There were around him most, though not quite all, of the trusty coadjutors whom his brother Henry had originally collected, or whom he himself had summoned. His position during the crisis about to supervene, resembled that of the Roman Senate after the battle of Cannæ, as set forth by the historian with vivid imagery—"The single torrent joined by a hundred lesser streams has swelled into a wide flood; and the object of our interest is a rock, now islanded amid the waters, and against which they dash furiously, as though they must needs sweep it away. But the rock stands unshaken; the waters become feebler, the rock seems to rise higher and higher; and the danger is passed away."

In May, 1857, he had as usual retired to his Himalayan retreat at Murri for the summer, anxious regarding the mutinous symptoms, which had appeared at various stations of the Native army in other provinces, but not in the Punjab proper. He knew his own province to be secure even against a revolt of the Native troops; his anxiety referred to his neighbours over whom he had no authority, and he hoped for the best respecting them. He had in April been suffering from neuralgia, and had even feared lest the distress and consequent weakness should drive him to relinquish his charge for a time. He had however decided to remain yet another year. His pain pursued him in the mountains. The paroxysm of an acute attack had been subdued by the use of aconite, which relieving the temples caused sharp anguish in the eyes,—when the fateful telegram came from Delhi. He rose from a sick bed to read the message which a telegraph clerk, with admirable presence of mind, despatched just before the wires were broken by the mutineers and the mob. He thus learnt, within a few hours of their occurrence, the striking and shocking events which had occurred there, the outbreak of the native soldiery, the murder of the Europeans, the momentary cessation of British rule, and in its place the assumption of kingly authority by the titular Moslem Emperor. Learning all this at least two days before the public of the Punjab could hear of it, he was able to take all necessary precautions civil, political, military, so that when the wondrous news should arrive the well-wishers of the Government might be encouraged and the evil-disposed abashed at finding that measures had actually been taken or were in hand. The excitement of battling with emergency seemed for a while to drive away the pain from his nerves, and to banish every sensation save that of pugnacity.

After the lapse of a generation who can now describe the dismay which for a moment chilled even such hearts as his, when the amazing news from Delhi was flashed across the land! For weeks indeed a still voice had been whispering in his ear that at the many stations held by Sepoys alone a revolt, if attempted, must succeed. But he had a right to be sure that wherever European troops were stationed, there no snake of mutiny would dare to rear its head and hiss. Here, however, he saw that the mutinous Sepoys had broken loose at Meerut, the very core of our military power in Hindostan, and had, in their flight to Delhi, escaped the pursuit of European cavalry, artillery and infantry. For them, too, he knew what an inestimable prize was Delhi, a large city, walled round with fortifications, and containing an arsenal-magazine full of munitions. It is ever important politically that European life should be held sacred by the Natives, and he was horror-stricken on learning that this sacredness had been atrociously violated. If British power depended partly on moral force, then here he felt a fatally adverse effect, for the rebellion started with a figure-head in the Great Mogul, veritably a name to conjure with in India. His feeling was momentarily like that of sailors on the outbreak of fire at sea, or on the crash of a collision. But if the good ship reeled under the shock, he steadied her helm and his men stood to their places.

Within three days he received the reports from his headquarters at Lahore, showing how Montgomery, as chief civil authority on the spot, had with the utmost promptitude carried to the commander of the troops there the telegraphic news from Delhi before the event could be known by letters or couriers, and had urged the immediate disarming of the Sepoys, how the commander had disarmed them with signal skill and success, and how the capital of the province had thus been rendered safe.

Murri being near the frontier, he was able to confer

personally with Herbert Edwardes, one of the greatest of his lieutenants, who was Commissioner of Peshawur, the most important station in the province next after Lahore itself. At Peshawur also he had John Nicholson, a pillar of strength.

During May and June he received reports of disaster daily in most parts of Northern India, and he knew that his own province, notwithstanding outward calm, was stirred with conflicting emotions inwardly.

The events of 1857 were so full of epic grandeur, their results so vast, their details so terrific, their incidents so complex, and the part which he played in connection with them was so important, that it is difficult to do justice to his achievements without entering upon a historic summary for which space cannot be allowed here. By reason of his conduct in the Punjab at this crisis, he has been hailed as the deliverer and the preserver of India. In an account of his life it is necessary at the very least to recapitulate, just thirty years after the event, the several acts, measures or proceedings of his which gave him a claim to this eminent title. All men probably know that he brought about a result of the utmost value to his country. It is well to recount the steps by which he reached this national goal.

From the recapitulation of things done under his direction and on his responsibility, it is not to be inferred that he alone did them. On the contrary, he had the suggestions, the counsel, the moral support, the energetic obedience of his subordinates, and the hearty co-operation of many military commanders who were not his subordinates. He always acknowledged the aid he thus received, as having been essential to any success that was attained. He had his share in the credit, and they had theirs severally and collectively. In the first enthusiasm of success, after the fall of Delhi in September, he wrote in a letter to Edwardes: "Few men, in a similar position, have had so many true and good supporters around him. But for them what could I have done?"

He was from the beginning of the crisis in May, 1857, left in his province, unsupported by all other parts of India save Scinde,—*penitus toto divisus orbe.* The temporary establishment of the rebel headquarters at Delhi divided him and the Punjab from North-Western India, cutting off all direct communication with Calcutta and the Governor-General. He did not for many weeks receive any directions by post or telegraph from Lord Canning. It was not till August that he received one important message from the Governor-General by the circuitous route of Bombay and Scinde, as will be seen hereafter. He was thus thrown absolutely on his own resources, a circumstance which had more advantages than drawbacks, as it enabled him to act with all his originality and individuality.

Thus empowered by the force of events, his action spread over a wide field, the complete survey of which would comprise many collateral incidents relating to many eminent persons and to several careers of the highest distinction. All that can be undertaken here is to state the principal heads of his proceedings as concerning his conduct individually, with the mention only of a few persons who were so bound up with him that they must be noticed in order to elucidate his unique position.

His first step was to confirm the prompt and decisive

measures taken by his lieutenants at Lahore (as already mentioned) under the spur of emergency, whereby the capital of the Punjab was placed beyond the reach of danger.

But he saw in an instant that the self-same danger of mutiny among the native troops, from which Lahore had been saved, menaced equally all the other military stations of the Punjab, namely Jullundur and Ferozepore, both in the basin of the Sutlej river, Sealkote on the Himalayan border, Mooltan commanding the approach to Scinde on the river-highway between the Punjab and the sea, Rawul-Pindi and Peshawur in the region of the Indus, Jhelum commanding the river of that name; at each of which stations a body of Sepoys, possibly mutinous, was stationed. Therefore he proposed that a movable column of European troops should be formed and stationed in a central and commanding position, ready to proceed at once to any station where mutiny might show itself among the Sepoys, to assist in disarming them or in beating them down should they rise in revolt, and to cut off their escape should they succeed in flying with arms in their hands. He procured in concert with the local military authorities the appointment of Neville Chamberlain to command this movable column, and then of John Nicholson, when Chamberlain was summoned to Delhi. There were many technical difficulties in completing this arrangement which indeed was vitally needful, but they were surmounted only by his masterful influence. Chamberlain was already well known to him from service on the Trans-Indus frontier. Nicholson was his nominee specially (having been originally brought forward by his brother Henry) and will be prominently mentioned hereafter. He was indeed instrumental in placing Nicholson in a position which proved of momentous consequence to the country in a crisis of necessity.

But too soon it became evident that his worst apprehensions regarding the Sepoys in the Punjab would be fulfilled. Then finding that no proclamation to the Sepoys was being issued by the Commander-in-Chief from Delhi, and that no message could possibly come from the Governor-General, he determined after consulting the local military authorities to issue a proclamation from himself as Chief Commissioner to the Sepoys in the Punjab, and to have it posted up at every cantonment or station. The most important sentences from it may be quoted here.

"Sepoys! I warn and advise you to prove faithful to your salt; faithful to the Government who have given your forefathers and you service for the last hundred years; faithful to that Government who, both in cantonments and in the field, have been careful of your welfare and interests, and who, in your old age, have given you the means of living comfortably in your homes. Those regiments which now remain faithful will receive the rewards due to their constancy; those soldiers who fall away now will lose their service for ever! It will be too late to lament hereafter when the time has passed by. Now is the opportunity of proving your loyalty and good faith. The British Government will never want for native soldiers. In a month it might raise 50,000 in the Punjab alone. You know well enough that the British Government have never interfered with your religion. The Hindoo temple and the Mahommedan mosque have both been respected by the English Government. It was but the other day that the Jumma mosque at Lahore, which the Sikhs had converted into a magazine, was restored to the Mahommedans."

Simultaneously under his directions, or with his sanction, several important forts, arsenals, treasuries and strategic positions, which had been more or less in the guardianship of the Sepoys, were swiftly transferred to the care of European troops, before mutiny had time to develope itself.

Soon it became necessary for him to urge, with as much secrecy as possible, the disarming of the Sepoys at nearly every station in the Punjab. This measure was successful at Peshawur, though with some bloodshed and other distressful events; at Rawul Pindi it was carried out under his own eye; at Mooltan a point of vital importance, it was executed brilliantly under provident arrangements which he was specially instrumental in suggesting. It was effected generally by the presence of European troops; at Mooltan, however, he was proud to reflect that it had been managed by Punjabi agency with the aid of some loyal Hindostanis. But at Ferozepore its success was partial only, at Jullundur the mutineers escaped through local incompetence, but the effects were mitigated by his arrangements. At Sealkote he had advised disarming before the European regiment was withdrawn to form the Movable Column already mentioned; nevertheless the military commanders tried to keep the Sepoys straight without disarming them, so when the mutiny did occur it could not be suppressed. He felt keenly the ill effects of this disaster brought about as it was by murderous treachery. But the mutineers were cut off with heavy loss by the Movable Column which he had organised. Space, indeed, forbids any attempt to describe the disarming of the Sepoys which was executed at his instance, or with his approval, throughout the Province. Once convinced that the Sepoys were intending, if not actual, mutineers, he gave his *mot d'ordre* to disarm, disarm; and this was the primary step in the path of safety.

Even then, however, at nearly every large station there were bodies of disarmed Sepoys, ripe for any mischief, who had to be guarded, and the guarding of them was a grave addition to his toils and anxieties; it was done however with success.

His anxiety for the future of Mooltan was acute, as that place commanded the only line of communication that remained open between the Punjab and India, and the only road of retreat in event of disaster. So help from the Bombay side was entreated; and he felt inexpressibly thankful when the Bombay European Fusiliers arrived at Mooltan speedily from Scinde, and when a camel-train was organised for military transport to that place from Kurrachi on the seaboard. He rendered heartfelt acknowledgments to Bartle Frere, to whose energy the speedy arrival of this much-needed reinforcement was due. Come what might, he would cling to Mooltan even to the bitterest end, as events had caused this place to be for a time the root of British power in the Punjab.

Almost his first care was to urge on the movement which was being made by the Commander-in-Chief, General Anson, who, assembling the European Regiments then stationed in the Himalayas near Simla and at Umballa, proposed to march upon Delhi. His immediate counsel to the Commander-in-Chief, from a political point of view—irrespective of the military considerations of which the General must be the judge

—was to advance. If, he argued, success in stopping the rebellion depended on moral as well as on physical force, then a forward movement would affect the public mind favourably, while inactivity must produce a corresponding depression; thus we could not possibly afford to stand still, and an advancing policy would furnish our only chance. Rejoiced to find that counsels of this character prevailed at the army headquarters then established between Simla and Umballa, and that the European force had its face turned straight towards Delhi, he set himself to help in finding transport, supplies and escort. The line of march lay along the high road from Umballa to Delhi about one hundred miles, so he helped with his civil and political resources to clear and pioneer the way. When the European force laid siege to Delhi, this road became the line of communication with the rear, the chain of connection between the combatants in camp on the Delhi ridge and the military base at Umballa; this line, then, he must keep open. Fortunately the adjoining districts belonged chiefly to Native princes, who had for many years been protected by the British power and now proved themselves thoroughly loyal; so he through his officers organised the troops and the establishments of these Native States to help the British troops in patrolling the road, provisioning the supply depôts, escorting the stores and materials for the army in the front.

The Sepoys having mutinied or been disarmed throughout the Punjab, it became instantly necessary to supply their place if possible by trustworthy Native troops; to this task he applied himself with the utmost skill and energy. He caused the flower of the Punjab

Frontier force, already mentioned in a preceding chapter, to be despatched with extraordinary expedition to Delhi. He raised fresh levies, with very suggestive aid from Edwardes at Peshawur, by selecting men from among the Sikhs and Moslems of the Punjab. He had them rapidly organised for service in every part of the country from Peshawur to Delhi. As these new troops were thus promptly formed, he kept a prudent eye on their total number. Finding this number was mounting to more than fifty thousand men of all arms, he stopped short, considering this to be the limit of safety, and he restrained the zeal of his lieutenants so as to prevent any undue or excessive number being raised. He from the first foresaw that the fresh Punjabi soldiery must not be too numerous, nor be allowed to feel that the physical force was on their side.

The selection of trustworthy Native officers for the new troops required much discrimination; but his personal knowledge of all eminent and well-informed Punjabis enabled him either to make the choice himself, or to obtain guidance in choosing.

It is hard to describe what a task he and his coadjutors had in order to provide this considerable force within a very few weeks—to raise and select trusty men from widely scattered districts, to drill, equip, clothe, arm and officer them, to discipline and organise them in marching order, to place them on garrison duty or despatch them for service in the field. A large proportion of them, too, must be mounted, and for these he had to collect horses.

Special care had to be taken by him for the watch and ward of the long frontier adjoining Afghanistan for several hundred miles, which border had been deprived of some of its best troops for service before Delhi. This critical task, too, he accomplished with entire success.

Further, one notable step was taken by him in respect to the Sepoy regiments. The Sepoys were for the most part Hindostanis, but in every corps there were some Sikhs or Punjabis; he caused these latter to be separated from their comrades and embodied in the newly-formed forces. Thus he saved hundreds of good men from being involved in mutiny.

Anticipating the good which would be exerted on the public mind by the sight of the forces of the Native States being employed under the British standard before Delhi, he accepted the offers of assistance from these loyal feudatories. Under his auspices, the Chiefs in the Cis-Sutlej States were among the first to appear in arms on the British side. Afterwards he arranged with the Maharaja of Jammu and Cashmere for the despatch of a contingent from those Himalayan regions to join the British camp at Delhi; and he deputed his brother Richard to accompany this contingent as political agent.

It was providentially fortunate for him and his that no sympathy existed between the Punjabis and the mutinous Sepoys, but on the contrary a positive antipathy. The Sepoys of the Bengal army who were mutineers nearly all belonged to Oude and Hindostan; the Punjabis regarded them as foreigners, and detested them ever since the first Sikh war, even disliking their presence in the Punjab; he was fully alive to this feeling, and made the very most of it for the good of the

British cause. He knew too that they hated Delhi as the city where their warrior-prophet Tegh Behadur had been barbarously put to death, and where the limbs of the dead martyr had been exposed on the ramparts. In the first instance the Punjabis regarded the mutinies as utter follies sure to bring down retribution, and they were glad to be among his instruments in dealing out punishment to the mutineers, and so "feeding fat their grudge" against them. They told him that the bread which the Sepoys had rejected would fall to the lot of the loyal Punjab. Thus he seized this great advantage instantly, and drove the whole force of Punjabi sentiment straight against the rebels, saying in effect as Henry V. said to his soldiers,

> "I see you stand like greyhounds in the slips,
> Straining upon the start. The game's afoot;
> Follow your spirit and upon this charge
> Cry, 'God for Harry, England, and St. George.'"

As outbreak after outbreak occurred, he pressed for the signal and condign punishment of the leaders, as a deterrent to those who might yet be wavering between duty and revolt. But this object having been secured, he instantly tried to temper offended justice with at least a partial clemency, lest men should be tempted to rebellion by despair. When batches of red-handed mutineers were taken prisoners, he would intercede so that the most guilty only should be blown from guns, and that the lives of the rest should be spared with a view to imprisonment. In such moments, he would support his appeal by invoking his officers to look into their consciences as before the Almighty. This solemn invocation—rarely uttered by him, though its sense was ever on his mind—attested the earnestness of his conviction.

By this time he and his were regarded as forming the military base of the operations against Delhi. Thither had he sent off many of his best troops and his ablest officers, besides stores and material. Prudential considerations had been duly brought to his notice in reference to the Punjab itself becoming denuded of its resources. But after weighing all this carefully yet rapidly, he decided that the claims of the British besiegers, encamped over against the rebellious Delhi, were paramount, and he acted on that decision.

Fortunately the arsenals and magazines in his province were fully supplied, and soon after the great outbreak in May a siege-train had been despatched to Delhi. But he knew that the siege was laid on one side only out of several sides, nothing like an investment being practicable as the besieged had perfect communication with their base in the rebellious Hindostan. So he prepared his province to supply the countless necessaries for the conduct of such a siege, against a city girdled with several miles of fortifications, possessing many internal resources which were further fed from the outside, and defended by disciplined rebels, who on rebelling had seized the treasure in the vaults, the ordnance and warlike stores in the magazine of the place. Thus for many weeks he sent convoy after convoy, even driblet after driblet, of miscellaneous ordnance stores, saddlery, tents, sand-bags and articles innumerable. For all this work a complete transport-train was organised under his orders, to ply daily on the road leading to the rear of the British forces before

Delhi. The vehicles, the animals for draught or for baggage, the bullocks, the camels, the elephants, were hired or purchased by him in his province and its dependencies. The drivers and riders were taken from the people in his jurisdiction, and they behaved towards their trusted master with steadiness and fidelity. He sorely needed the public moneys available in the Punjab for his own operations there; still out of them he spared large sums to be sent to Delhi, knowing that from nowhere else but the Punjab could a rupee be obtained by the besiegers. If a few native troops of a special character, such as sappers and pioneers, were required, he would select old soldiers of the late Sikh armies and despatch them to the siege. As the operations of the siege advanced, a second train of heavy guns was needed, and this he sent in the nick of time by transport collected in the Punjab. He was in constant correspondence with the commanders before Delhi, and thus knew their needs, their perils, and their chances. They sent him all their requisitions, and looked upon him as their military base. It may be said that he never refused a requisition either for men, money or means; and that he hardly ever failed to fulfil any request with which compliance had been promised.

It is hard to paint the picture of his work in these days, because the canvas has to be crowded with many diverse incidents and policies. At one moment he cries in effect—disarm the rebel Sepoys, disarm them quick, inflict exemplary punishment, stamp out mutiny, pursue, cut off retreat—at another, spare, spare, temper judgment with discriminating clemency—at another, advance, advance, raise levies, place men wherever wanted—at another, hold fast, don't do too much, by an excessive number of new men a fresh risk is run—at another, seize such and such strategic points, guard such and such river-passages—at another, break up this or that pontoon bridge to prevent the enemy crossing—at another, press forward the transport, push on the supplies—at all moments, put a cheerful as well as a bold face even on the worst, for the sake of moral effect. He unravelled the threads of countless transactions, collated the thick-coming reports from all the districts, and noted the storm-warnings at every point of his political compass. His warfare with the rebels and mutineers was offensive as well as defensive. His word always was, attack, attack, so that the people, seeing this aggressive attitude, might not lose heart. His energy in these days might be called resplendent, as it was all-pervading, life-infusing, and ranged in all directions with the broadest sweep. But he recked little of glory, for the crisis was awful.

It may possibly be asked what the Punjab and the empire would have done, had he at this time fallen or been stricken down. Such questions, however, imply scant justice to him and his system; and he would have taken them as sorry compliments. He had ever so laboured that his work might live after him. Around him were several leaders capable of commanding events or directing affairs; and under him was an admirable band of officers civil and military, trained under his eye, on whom his spirit rested, and who were ready to follow his lieutenant or successor even as they had followed him.

Then financial difficulty stared him in the face, in

respect not only of the normal but also of the abnormal expenses in the Punjab. It will have been understood from a preceding chapter that his provincial treasury, though sufficing for the expenses of the Province and for its share in the military expenditure, was not full enough to meet the entire cost of the army cantoned in the province for the defence of the empire generally. Up to the end of April in this year, he had drawn large supplies in cash regularly from the treasuries in Hindostan and Bengal. But from May onwards these supplies were cut off, and he was left to provide money not only for the old charges of the Province, but also for the new charges on account of the extraordinary measures which had been adopted. He therefore raised loans of money locally, and moral pressure had to be applied to the Native capitalists. He observed that these men, who are usually ready and loyal and are bound to us by many ties, now hung back and showed closefistedness. This he regarded as an index of their fears for the issue of the desperate struggle in which we were engaged. He also invited subscriptions from the Native Princes and Chiefs. Having raised large sums in this way, he was able to keep the various treasuries open, and to avoid suspending payment anywhere. His first care, after the restoration of peace and plenty, was to repay the temporary creditors.

As the news from the British forces before Delhi grew more and more unfavourable during June and July, he reflected, with characteristic forethought, on the steps to be taken in the event of disaster in that quarter. Among other things he apprehended that it might become necessary to retire from Peshawur, so that the large

European force cantoned there might be concentrated for the defence of the Province. This apprehension of his caused much discussion subsequently, and is likely to be fraught with historic interest. He thus expressed himself in a letter to Edwardes on June 9th.

"I think we must look ahead and consider what should be done in the event of disaster at Delhi. My decided opinion is that, in that case, we must concentrate. All our safety depends on this. If we attempt to hold the whole country, we shall be cut up in detail. The important points in the Punjab are Peshawur, Mooltan, and Lahore, including Umritsur. But I do not think that we can hold Peshawur and the other places also, in the event of disaster. We could easily retire from Peshawur early in the day. But at the eleventh hour, it would be difficult, perhaps impossible."

On the following day, June 10th, he wrote in the same strain to Lord Canning, but adding that he would not give up Peshawur so long as he saw a chance of success. He asked that a telegram might be sent to him by the circuitous route of Bombay (the only route then open) containing one of two alternative replies—"Hold on to Peshawur to the last,"—or, "You may act as may appear expedient in regard to Peshawur." Very soon he received Edwardes's reply that, "With God's help we can and will hold Peshawur, let the worst come to the worst." On June 18th after a conversation with Nicholson, who was utterly opposed to retiring from Peshawur, he wrote to Edwardes repeating that in the event of a great disaster such retirement might be necessary. No reply being received from Lord Canning, he prepared to act upon this view as the extremity of the crisis seemed to loom nearer and nearer during June and July. He reiterated his views in two despatches to the Governor-General, one at the end of June, the other at the end of July. But by August 1st public intelligence from India and England reached him, modifying favourably, though it did not remove, the crisis. On the 7th of that month he received Lord Canning's reply, "Hold on to Peshawur to the last." He immediately writes to Edwardes: "The Governor-General bids me hold on to the last at Peshawur. I do not, however, now think that we shall be driven to any extremity. The tide is turning very decidedly against the mutineers at Delhi." This episode evinces his moral courage and single-mindedness in all that concerned the public safety, for he must have well known that proposals for retirement were invidious, and might prove unpopular with many of his supporters.

When he spoke about the turning of the tide he alluded partly to the news, which was slowly travelling to the Punjab from England, regarding the despatch to India of mighty reinforcements of European troops. These would not indeed reach him in time, but the knowledge nerved him to hold out, as every day gained was a step towards victory.

On August 6th he heard at last the tidings of his brother's death at Lucknow, from a mortal wound while in bed from the bursting of a shell which had penetrated the chamber. Immediately he telegraphed to Edwardes, "My brother Henry was wounded on July 2nd, and died two days afterwards." The same day he wrote to Edwardes, "Henry died like a good soldier in discharge of his duty; he has not left an abler or better soldier behind him; his loss just now will be a national calamity."

In the middle of July he left Murri and proceeded to Lahore, where he remained at his headquarters till the end of the crisis. There he took counsel daily with Montgomery and Macleod, the very men on whose courageous alacrity he most relied for the despatch of public business. For four weary months he sustained British authority in the Punjab on the whole from end to end, notwithstanding the agitation caused by several mutinous outbreaks of the Sepoys, and despite several desperate attempts at insurrection in some districts. He kept down the disorder, which was but too ready to upheave itself when the worst example was being set in neighbouring provinces, and while stories of distant disasters were flying about. He extinguished every flame that burst forth. Having under him a matchless staff of officers, civil, political, military, he set before them all by his own bearing and conduct an example which they nobly followed. Thus throughout the crisis he maintained, intact and uninterrupted, the executive power in the civil administration, the collection of the revenue to the uttermost farthing, the operations of the judicial courts, the action of the police. He saw, not only the suppression of violent crime, but also the most peaceful proceedings conducted, such as the dispensing of relief to the sick and the attendance of children at school. He felt that during the suspense of the public mind, a sedative is produced by the administrative clock-work moving in seconds, minutes, hours of precious time won for the British cause. He was ruling over the Native population, which was indeed the most martial among all the races in India, but which also had been beaten and conquered by British prowess within living memory. He now took care that the British prestige should be preserved in their minds, and that the British star should still before their eyes be in the ascendant. Knowing them to have that generosity which always belongs to brave races, he determined to trust them as the surest means of ensuring their fidelity. Therefore he chose the best fighting men amongst them to aid their late conquerors in the Punjab, and to re-conquer the rebellious Hindostan. He knew that one way of keeping the fiercer and more restless spirits out of mischief was to hurl them at the common foe.

But the months wore on from May to September while Delhi remained untaken, and he knew that week by week the respect of the Punjab people, originally high, for the British Government, was being lowered by the spectacle of unretrieved disaster. He felt also that the patience of the evil-disposed, which had been happily protracted, must be approaching nearer and nearer to the point of exhaustion. He saw that sickness was creeping over the robust frame of the body politic, and that the symptoms of distemper, which were day by day appearing in the limbs, might ere long extend to the vital organs. He learned, from intercepted correspondence, the sinister metaphors which were being applied to what seemed to be the sinking state of the British cause—such as "many of the finest trees in the garden have fallen," or "white wheat is scarce and country produce abundant," or "hats are hardly to be seen while turbans are countless."

Yet it was evident to him that the force before Delhi in August would not suffice to recapture the place, although he had sent all the reinforcements which could properly be spared from the Punjab. But if Delhi should remain untaken, the certainty of disturbance throughout the Punjab presented itself to him. He must therefore make one supreme effort to so strengthen the Delhi camp that an assault might be soon delivered. This he could do by despatching thither the one last reserve which the Punjab possessed, namely Nicholson's movable column. This was a perilous step to take, and his best officers, as in duty bound, pointed out its perils; still he resolved to adopt it. If the column should go, grave risk would indeed be incurred for the Punjab, but then there was a chance of Delhi being taken, and of the Punjab being preserved; if the column should not go, then Delhi would not be taken, and in that case the Punjab must sooner or later be lost; and he had finally to decide between these two alternatives. His intimate acquaintance with the people taught him that if a general rising should occur in consequence of the British failing to take Delhi, then the presence of the movable column in the Punjab would not save the Province. This was the crisis not only in his career, but also in the fate of the Punjab and of Delhi with Hindostan. He decided in favour of action, not only as the safer of two alternatives, but as the only alternative which afforded any hope of safety. He was conscious that this particular decision was fraught with present risk to the Punjab, which had hardly force enough for self-preservation. But he held that the other alternative must ultimately lead to destruction. His decision thus formed had to be followed by rapid action, for sickness at the end of summer and beginning of autumn was literally decimating the European force before Delhi week by week; and even each day as it passed appreciably lessened the fighting strength. So the column marched with all speed for Delhi; and then he had sped his last bolt. In his own words, he had poured out the cup of his resources to the last drop.

Thus denuded, his position was critical indeed. He had but four thousand European soldiers remaining in the Punjab, and of these at least one half were across the Indus near the Khyber Pass. Several strategic points were held by detachments only of European troops, and he could not but dread the sickly season then impending. He had eighteen thousand Sepoys to watch, of whom twelve thousand had been disarmed and six thousand still had their arms. Of his newly-raised Punjabis the better part had been sent to Delhi; but a good part remained to do the necessary duties in the Punjab; and what if they should come to think that the physical force was at their disposal?

The sequel formed one of the bright pages in British annals, and amply justified the responsibility which he had incurred. The column arrived in time to enable the British force to storm and capture Delhi; and he mourned, as a large-hearted man mourns, over the death of Nicholson in the hour of triumph. He declared that Nicholson, then beyond the reach of human praise, had done deeds of which the memory could never perish so long as British rule should endure.

His relief was ineffable when tidings came that Delhi had been stormed, the mutineers defeated and expelled, the so-called Emperor taken prisoner, the fugitive rebels pursued, the city and the surrounding districts restored to British rule. To his ear the knell of the great rebellion had sounded. He could not but feel proud at the thought that this result had been achieved without any reinforcement whatever from England. But he was patriotically thankful to hear of the succour despatched by England, through Palmerston her great Minister—some fifty thousand men in sailing vessels by a long sea-route round the Cape of Good Hope, full twelve thousand miles in a few months, by an effort unparalleled in warlike annals.

While the peril was at its height, his preoccupation almost drowned apprehension. But when the climax was over, he was awe-struck on looking back on the narrowness of the escape. He recalled to mind the desperate efforts which he and his men had put forth. But he was profoundly conscious that, humanly speaking, no exertions of this nature were adequate to cope with the frightful emergency which had lasted so long as to strain his resources almost to breaking. The fatuity, which often haunts criminals, had affected the mutineers and the rebel leaders; error had dogged their steps, and their unaccountable oversights had, in his opinion, contributed to the success of the British cause. He used to say that their opportunity would, if reasonably used, have given them the mastery; but that they with their unreason threw away its advantages, and that in short had they pursued almost any other course than that which they did pursue, the British flag must have succumbed. Thus regarding with humility the efforts of which the issue had been happy, he felt truly, and strove to inspire others with, a sentiment of devout thankfulness to the God of battles and the Giver of all victory.

He believed that if Delhi had not fallen, and if the

tension in the Punjab had been prolonged for some more months, even for some more weeks, the toils of inextricable misfortune would have closed round his administration. The frontier tribes would, he thought, have marched upon half-protected districts, and would have been joined by other tribes in the interior of the province. One military station after another would have been abandoned by the British, so that the available forces might be concentrated at Lahore the capital; and finally there would have been a retreat, with all the European families and a train of camp-followers, from Lahore down the Indus valley towards the seaboard. Then, as he declared, no Englishman would for a whole generation have been seen in the Punjab, either as a conqueror or as a ruler.

As to his share in the recapture of Delhi, the testimony may be cited of an absolutely competent witness, Lord Canning, a man of deliberate reflection, who always measured his words, and who wrote some time after the event when all facts and accounts had been collated, thus:

> "Of what is due to Sir John Lawrence himself no man is ignorant. Through him Delhi fell, and the Punjab, no longer a weakness, becomes a source of strength. But for him, the hold of England over Upper India would have had to be recovered at a cost of English blood and treasure which defies calculation."

Delhi had heretofore belonged not to the Punjab, but to the North-Western Provinces; on being re-taken by the British in September, it was, together with the surrounding territory, made over during October to his care and jurisdiction. Having removed all traces of the recent storm from the surface of the Punjab, he proceeded to Delhi in order to superintend in person the restoration of law and order there. Before starting, he helped the Commander-in-Chief (Sir Colin Campbell, afterwards Lord Clyde) in arranging that the Punjabi troops, raised during the summer, should be despatched southwards beyond Delhi for the reconquest of Hindostan and Oude. He also wrote to the Secretary of State entreating that his good officers might be remembered in respect of rewards and honours. His wife's health had failed, and he had seen her start for a river voyage down the Indus on her way to England. He was at this time very anxious on her account, and would say, what avail would all worldly successes and advantages be to him if he should lose her? So he started for Delhi sore at heart; but he received better accounts of her, and his spirits rose with the approach of the winter season, which in Upper India always serves as a restorative to the European constitution.

Then crossing the Sutlej, he entered the friendly States of the Protected Sikh Chiefs, who had been saved by the British from absorption under Runjit Sing, the Lion of Lahore, and whose loyalty had shown like white light during the darkest days of recent months. Having exchanged with them all the heartiest congratulations, he passed on to Delhi and to the scenes of his younger days. With what emotions must he have revisited the imperial city—to all men associated with the majestic march of historic events, but to him fraught with the recollections of that period of life which to the eye of memory almost always seems bright,—yet just emerging from a condition of tragic horror, the darkness of which had been lighted up by the deeds of British prowess and endurance. As he rode through the desolate bazaars, the half-deserted alleys, the thoroughfares traversed by bodies of men under arms but no longer crowded with bustling traffic—he must have grieved over the fate which the rebellious city had brought on itself. His penetrating insight taught him that in this case, as in nearly all similar cases, the innocent suffer with the guilty, and the peace-loving, kindly-disposed citizens are involved in the sanguinary retribution which befalls the turbulent and the blood-seeking. He found the fair suburbs razed, the fortifications partly dismantled, the famous Muri bastion half-shattered by cannonading, the classic Cashmere Gate riddled with gunshot, the frontage of houses disfigured by musketry, the great Moslem place of worship temporarily turned into a barrack for Hindoo troops. The noble palace of the Moguls alone remained intact, and he passed under the gloomy portal where some of the first murders were perpetrated on the morning of the great mutiny, and so entered the court-yard where the Christian prisoners of both sexes had been put to the sword. Then he proceeded to the inner sanctum of the palace to see his imperial prisoner, the last of the Great Moguls. He could not but eye with pity this man, the remnant of one of the most famous dynasties in human annals, reduced to the dregs of misery and humiliation in the extremity of old age. Yet he regarded with stern reserve a prisoner who, though illustrious by antecedents and drawn irresistibly into the vortex of rebellion, was accused of murder in ordering the execution of the European captives. He was resolved that the ex-emperor should be arraigned on a capital charge, and abide the verdict of a criminal tribunal.

He knew, however, that by the speedy restoration of the civil authority, the harried, plundered, partly devastated city would revive; for the presence of troops in large bodies and their camp-followers created a demand, which the peasants would supply if they could bring their goods to market without fear of marauding on the way, and expose them for sale without molestation. He thus saw the closed shops reopened, the untenanted houses re-occupied, the empty marts beginning once more to be crowded; though the city must wear the air of mourning for a long while before the brilliancy and gaiety of past times should re-appear.

The re-establishment of police authority for current affairs, and of civil justice between man and man, formed the easiest and pleasantest portion of his task. A more grave and anxious part devolved upon him respecting the treatment of persons who were already in confinement for, or might yet be accused of, participation in the late rebellion. He learned that the rebellion, in itself bad enough, had been aggravated, indeed blackened, by countless acts of contumely, treachery and atrocity; that the minds of the European officers, after the endurance of such evils in the inclemency of a torrid climate, had become inflamed and exasperated; that the retribution had not only been most severe on those who were guilty in the first degree, but also on those who were guilty only in the second or the third degree; and that, in the haste of the time, those whose misconduct had been passive, and even those who had been but slightly to blame, were mixed up with the active criminals in indiscriminating condemnation. He would make every allowance for his countrymen who had borne the burden and heat of an awful day, but he was there to overlook and see that they were not hurried away by excitability into proceedings which their after judgment could never approve. Though rigid in striking down those who were *in flagrante delicto*, and were actively engaged in murderous rebellion, yet he would hold his hand as soon as the stroke had effected its legitimate purpose. While the emergency lasted he would not hesitate in the most summary measures of repression; it was the life of the assailed against the life of their assailants. But as soon as the emergency had been overcome, he was for showing mercy, for exercising discrimination, for putting an end to summary procedure, and for substituting a criminal jurisdiction with a view to calm and deliberate judgment. On his arrival at Delhi there were the most pressing reasons for enforcing this principle, and forthwith he enforced it with all his energy and promptitude. He immediately organised special tribunals for the disposal of all cases which were pending in respect of the late rebellion, or which might yet be brought forward. He took care that no man thus charged should be tried, executed, or otherwise punished summarily, but should be brought to regular trial, without delay indeed, but on the other hand without undue haste, and should not suffer without having had all fair chances of exculpating himself. All this may appear a matter of course to us now after the lapse of a generation, but it was hard indeed for him to accomplish then, immediately after the subsidence of the political storm; and it needed all his persistency and firmness.

It then devolved upon him to inquire officially into the circumstances of the sudden outbreak in May, 1857, and of the subsequent events. His inquiries showed that the Sepoys had been tampered with for some weeks previously, but not for any long time; that they were tempted to join the conspiracy by the fact of their being left without the control of European troops, and in command of such a centre as Delhi, with such a personality as the ex-emperor; all which lessons he took to heart as warnings for the future. He found that the city had been plundered of all the wealth which had been accumulated during half a century of secure commerce and prosperity under British rule; but that the plundering had been committed by the mob or by miscellaneous robbers, and not by the victorious soldiery Native or European. He was rejoiced to ascertain that on the whole the European soldiery were free from any imputation of plundering, intemperance, violence, or maltreatment of the inhabitants, despite the temptations which beset them, the provocation which they had received, and the hardships they had suffered.

Having assured himself that the stream of British rule at Delhi had begun to flow peacefully in its pristine channel, he returned to Lahore by daily marches in February, 1858. The weather was bright, the climate invigorating, the aspect of affairs inspiriting; and his health was fairly good. It was on this march that he caused a despatch to be prepared, at the instance of Edwardes at Peshawar, regarding the attitude of the

British Government in India towards Christianity. The fact of the mutinies beginning with a matter relating to caste and its prejudices, had drawn the attention of the authorities to the practical evils of the Hindoo system; the flames of rebellion had been fanned by Moslem fanaticism; the minds of all Europeans had been drawn towards their Almighty Preserver by the contemplation of deliverance from peril; thus the thoughts of men were turned towards Christianity; and he was specially disposed to follow this train of reflection. He little anticipated the influence which this despatch was destined to exercise on public opinion in England.

His carefulness in repaying the temporary loans, raised locally during the crisis, has already been mentioned. But there was another debt of honour to be discharged by him; for the Native states and chiefs, who had stood by us under the fire of peril, were to be rewarded. This he effected, with the sanction of the Governor-General, by allotting to them the estates confiscated for murderous treason or overt rebellion. He desired that the British Government should not benefit by these just and necessary confiscations, but that the property, forfeited by the disloyal, should be handed over to the loyal.

Thus he returned to Lahore, and thence went on to the Murri mountains in May, 1858, where he might have hoped to enjoy rest after a year of labour unprecedented even in his laborious life. But now a new danger began to arrest his attention. During the year just passed, from May 1857 to the corresponding month of 1858, his policy had been to organise Punjabi troops in place of the Sepoy force mutinous or disarmed, then to employ them for helping the European army in re-conquering the north-western provinces, and especially in re-capturing Lucknow. His Punjabis indeed were almost the only troops, except the Ghoorkas, employed with the European army in these important operations. Right loyally had they done their work, and well did they deserve to share in the honours of victory. They naturally were proud of the triumphs in which they had participated. They had a right to be satisfied with their own conduct. But they began to feel a sense of their own importance also. They had done much for the British Government, and might be required to do still more. Then they began to wonder whether the Government could do without them. These thoughts, surging in their minds, begat danger to the State. Information was received to the effect that Sikh officers of influence, serving in Oudh, were saying that they had helped to restore British power, and why should they not now set up a kingdom for themselves. These ideas were beginning to spread among the Punjabi troops serving not only in Oude and the north-western provinces, but also in the Punjab itself, even as far as the frontier of Afghanistan. All this showed that the hearts even of brave, and on the whole good, men may be evilly affected by pride and ambition or by a sense of overgrown power. Thus the very lessons of the recent mutinies were being taught again, and there was even a risk lest that terrible history should repeat itself. The Punjabis in truth were becoming too powerful for the safety of the State. So Lawrence had to exert all his provident skill in checking the growth of this dangerous power, and in so arranging that at no vital point or strategic situation should the Punjabis have a position of mastery.

The situation in the Punjab, too, was aggravated by the presence of considerable bodies of disarmed Sepoys still remaining at some of the large stations, who had to be guarded, and who on two occasions rose and broke out in a menacing manner.

While at Murri and on his way thither he caused a report to be drawn up for the Supreme Government regarding the events of 1857 in the Punjab, awarding praise, commendation, acknowledgment, to the civil and military officers of all ranks and grades for their services, meting out carefully to each man his due. He considered also the causes of this wondrous outbreak, as concerning not only his province but other parts of India, and as affecting the policy of the British Government in the East. He did not pay much heed to the various causes which had been ingeniously assigned in many well informed quarters. Some of these causes might, he thought, prove fanciful; others might be real more or less, but in so far as they were real they were only subsidiary. The affair of the greased cartridges, which has become familiar to History, was in his judgment really a provocative cause. It was, he said, the spark that fell upon, and so ignited, a combustible mass; but the question was, what made the mass combustible? There was, he felt, one all-pervading cause, pregnant with instruction for our future guidance. The Sepoy army, he declared, had become too powerful; they came to know that the physical force of the country was with them; the magazines and arsenals were largely, the fortresses partially, the treasuries wholly, in their keeping. They thought that they could at will upset the British Government and set up one of their own in its place; and this thought of theirs might, as he would remark, have proved correct, had not the Government obtained a mighty reinforcement from England, of which they could not form any calculation or even any idea. It was the sense of power, as he affirmed repeatedly, that induced the Sepoys to revolt. In the presence of such a cause as this, it availed little with him to examine subsidiary causes, the existence or the absence of which would have made no appreciable difference in the result. Neither did he undertake to discuss historically the gradual process whereby this excessive power fell into the hands of the Sepoys. The thing had happened, it ought not to have happened; that was practically enough for him; it must never, he said, be allowed to happen again. He took care that in his Province and its Dependencies, every strategic point, stronghold, arsenal, vantage-ground, even every important treasury, should be under the guardianship of European soldiers. He also provided that at every large station or cantonment, and at every central city, the physical force should be manifestly on the side of the Europeans. Though he reposed a generous confidence in the Native soldiery up to a certain point, and felt gratitude and even affection towards them for all that they had done under his direction, still he would no longer expose them to the fatal temptation caused by a consciousness of having the upper hand.

In reference to the Mutinies, he thought that the system of promotion by seniority to high military commands had been carried too far in the Indian Army.

There would always be difficulties in altering that system, but he held that unless such obstacles could be surmounted, the British Government in the East must be exposed to unexpected disasters occasionally, like thunderbolts dropping from the sky. Despite the warning from the Caubul losses of 1842, which arose mainly from the fault of the Commander, he noticed that the Meerut disaster of 1857 at this very time was owing again to failure on the local Commander's part, and a similar misfortune, though in a far lesser degree, occurred soon afterwards in the Punjab itself at Jullundur from the same cause. Incompetency in the Commander, he would say, neutralises the merits of the subordinates: there had been vigorous and skilful officers at Caubul, at Meerut, at Jullundur,—but all their efforts were in vain by reason of weakness in the man at the helm.

Soon were honours and rewards accorded to him by his Sovereign and the Government. He was promoted in the Order of the Bath from the rank of Knight Commander to that of Grand Cross. He was created a Baronet and a Privy Councillor. A special annuity of £2000 a year was granted him by the East India Company from the date when he should retire from the service. The emoluments, though not as yet the status, of a Lieutenant-Governor were accorded to him. He also received the Freedom of the City of London.

He marched from his Himalayan retreat at Murri during the autumn of 1858, with impaired health and an anxious mind. He trusted that the time had come when he might with honour and safety resign his high office. He knew that physically he ought to retire as soon as his services could be spared. He had every reason to hope for a speedy and happy return to his home in England. Yet he was not in really good spirits. Perhaps he felt the reaction which often supervenes after mental tension too long protracted. Partly from his insight into causes which might produce trouble even in the Punjab, and even after the general pacification of the disturbed regions, partly also from his natural solicitude that nothing untoward should occur to detain him beyond the beginning of 1859—he was nervously vigilant. After leaving Murri he crossed the Indus at Attok and revisited Peshawur. But neuralgia pursued him as he marched. At this time the royal proclamation of the assumption by the Queen of the direct government of India had arrived, and he wished to read it on horseback to the troops at Peshawur; but he performed the task with difficulty owing to the pain in his face. Once more from the citadel height he watched the crowded marts, rode close to the gloomy mouth of the Khyber Pass, and wondered at the classic stronghold of Attok as it overhangs the swift-flowing Indus.

As he crossed the Indus for the last time, towards the end of 1858, and rode along its left bank, that is on the Punjab side of the river, he gazed on the deep and rapid current of the mighty stream. That he held to be a real barrier which no enemy, advancing from the West upon India, could pass in the face of a British force. He noticed the breezy uplands overhanging the river on the east, and said that there the British defenders ought to be stationed. His mind reverted to the question, already raised by him in the summer of 1857, regarding the relinquishment of Peshawur. And he proposed to make over that famous valley to the Afghans, as its retention, in his view, was causing loss and embarrassment instead of gain and advantage to the British Government. The position was exposed to fierce antagonists and its occupation was in consequence costly; in it was locked up a European force which would be better employed elsewhere; that force had been decimated by the fever prevailing every autumn in the valley; the political and strategic advantages of the situation were purchased at too heavy a price, too severe a sacrifice; those advantages were possessed equally by Attok or any post on the Indus at a lesser cost. These were some of the arguments uppermost in his mind. The seasons had been even more insalubrious than usual, and he was grieved at the wear and tear of European life, the drain of European strength, in the valley. The transfer of a fertile and accessible territory to the Amir of Caubul would, he thought, give us a real hold upon the Afghans. It was not that he had any faith in the gratitude of the Afghans on the cession of Peshawur, which indeed they regard as a jewel and an object of the heart's desire; but if after the cession they should ever misbehave, then they could easily be punished by our re-occupation of the valley, and the knowledge that such punishment would be possible must, he conceived, bind them to our interests. Notwithstanding this deliberate opinion, which he deemed it his duty to record, the prevailing view among British authorities was then, and still is, in favour of retaining Peshawur as a political and strategic post of extraordinary value. Having submitted an opinion which was not accepted, he refrained from raising the question any further. At this time on the morrow, as it were, after the war of the Mutinies, he could hardly have anticipated that within one generation, or thirty years, the railway at more points than one would be advanced up to this Frontier, and that the Indus, then deemed a mighty barrier, would be a barrier no longer, being spanned by two bridges equally mighty, one at Attok in the Punjab, the other at Sukkur in Scinde, and perhaps by a third at Kalabagh. To those who can vividly recall the events of this time, the subsequent march of affairs in India is wonderful.

By the end of 1858 he had received the kind remonstrances of the Governor-General, Lord Canning, in regard to his leaving the Punjab. But he replied that if the public safety admitted of his going, he was bound from ill health to go. Indeed he needed relief, as the neuralgia continued at intervals to plague him. He had always a toil-worn, sometimes even a haggard, look. Despite occasional flashes of his vivacity or scintillations of his wit, his manner often indicated depression. He no longer walked or rode as much as formerly. As he had been in his prime a good and fast rider, the riding would be a fair test of his physical condition.

At this time the Punjab and its Dependencies, including the Delhi territory, were at last formed into a Lieutenant-Governorship, and he received the status and title of a position which he had long filled with potent reality. This measure, which formerly would have been of great use in sparing him trouble and labour, now came quite too late to be any boon to him in this respect. In view of his departure at the beginning of the coming year, 1859, he had secured the succession for his old friend and comrade, Montgomery, who had for some months been Chief-Commissioner of Oude.

Before leaving his post he was present at a ceremonial which marks an epoch in the material development of his province; for he turned the first sod of the first railway undertaken in the Punjab which was destined to connect its capital Lahore with Mooltan, Scinde, and the seaboard at Kurrachi.

Then he received a farewell address from his officers, civil and military, who had been eye-witnesses of all his labours, cares, perils and successes. The view taken by these most competent observers, most of whom were present during the time of disturbance, was thus set forth, and theirs is really evidence of the most direct and positive description.

"Those among us who have served with the Punjabi troops know how, for years, while the old force was on the frontier, you strove to maintain that high standard of military organisation, discipline and duty, of which the fruits were manifest when several regiments were, on the occurrence of the Bengal mutinies, suddenly summoned to serve as auxiliaries to the European forces, before Delhi, in Oude, in Hindostan,—on all which occasions they showed themselves worthy to be the comrades of Englishmen; how you, from the commencement, aided in maintaining a military police, which, during the crisis of 1857, proved itself to be the right arm of the civil power. They know how largely you contributed to the raising and forming of the new Punjabi force, which, during the recent troubles, did so much to preserve the peace within the Punjab itself, and which has rendered such gallant service in most parts of the Bengal Presidency. All those among us who are military officers, know how, when the Punjab was imperilled and agitated by the disturbances in Hindostan, you, preserving a unison of accord with the military authorities, maintained internal tranquillity, and held your own with our allies and subjects, both within and without the border; how, when the fate of Northern India depended on the capture of Delhi, you, justly appreciating the paramount importance of that object, and estimating the lowest amount of European force with which the Punjab could be held, applied yourself incessantly to despatching men, material, and treasure for the succour of our brave countrymen engaged in the siege ; how indeed you created a large portion of the means for carrying on that great operation, and devoted thereto all the available resources of the Punjab to the utmost degree compatible with safety."

In his reply, two passages are so characteristic that they may be quoted. He modestly recounts at least one among the mainsprings of his success, thus:

"I have long felt that in India of all countries, the great object of the Government should be to secure the services of able, zealous, and high-principled officials. Almost any system of administration, with such instruments, will work well. Without such officers, the best laws and regulations soon degenerate into empty forms. These being my convictions, I have striven, to the best of my ability, and with all the power which my position and personal influence could command, to bring forward such men. Of the many officers who have served in the Punjab, and who owe their present position, directly or indirectly, to my support, I can honestly affirm that I know not one who has not been chosen as the fittest person available for the post he occupies. In no one instance have I been guided in my choice by personal considerations, or by the claims of patronage. If my administration, then, of the Punjab is deserving of encomium, it is mainly on this account, and assuredly, in thus acting, I have reaped a rich reward. Lastly, it is with pleasure that I acknowledge how much I have been indebted to the military authorities in this Province for the cordiality and consideration I have ever received at their hands."

Further, he thus describes the conduct of the European soldiers under the severe conditions of the time—

"I thank the officers and men of the British European regiments serving in the Punjab, for the valour and endurance which they evinced during the terrible struggle. The deeds, indeed, need no words of mine to chronicle their imperishable fame. From the time that the English regiments, cantoned in the Simla hills, marched for Delhi in the burning month of May, 1857, exposure to the climate, disease and death under every form in the field, were their daily lot. Great as were the odds with which they had to combat, the climate was a far more deadly enemy than the mutineers.

"In a very few weeks, hundreds of brave soldiers were stricken down by fever, dysentery, and cholera. But their surviving comrades never lost their spirits. To the last they faced disease and death with the utmost fortitude. The corps which remained in the Punjab to hold the country, evinced a like spirit and similar endurance. Few in numbers, in a strange country, and in the presence of many enemies who only lacked the opportunity to break out, these soldiers maintained their discipline, constancy and patience."

Immediately afterwards, that is in the beginning of February, 1859, he started from Lahore, homeward bound, and steaming down the Indus arrived at Kurrachi. There near the Indus mouth he delighted in this cool and salubrious harbour, which, though not so capacious as some harbours, might, he knew, prove of infinite value hereafter, in the event of Britain having to stand in battle array on her Afghan frontier. There also he exchanged the friendliest greetings with Bartle Frere, the only external authority with whom he had been in communication throughout the crisis, and from whom he had received most useful co-operation. Thence he sailed for Bombay, which was still under the governorship of Lord Elphinstone, who had rendered valuable aid to the Punjab during the war. Bombay was then by no means the fair and noble capital that it now is; still he admired its land-locked basin, one of the finest harbours in the world, where fleets of war and of commerce may ride secure. He avoided public receptions so far as possible, and shortly proceeded by the mail steamer to England, where he arrived during the month of April. It may be well here to note that he was then only forty-eight years of age.

After the lapse of just one generation, time is already beginning to throw its halo over his deeds in 1857; the details are fading while the main features stand out in bolder and bolder relief. There is a monument to him in the minds of men;

> "And underneath is written,
> In letters all of gold,
> How valiantly he kept the Bridge
> In the brave days of old."

Doubtless this is not the last crisis which British India will have to confront and surmount; other crises must needs come, and in them the men of action will look back on his example. For the British of the future in India the prophet of Britain may say what was said for Rome;

> "And there, unquenched through ages
> Like Vesta's sacred fire,
> Shall live the spirit of thy nurse,
> The spirit of thy sire."

CHAPTER VIII

SOJOURN IN ENGLAND

1859-1864

IN the spring of 1859 John Lawrence took up his residence in London, with his wife and his family, now consisting of seven children. He assumed charge of his office as a member of the Council of India in Whitehall, to which he had been nominated by Lord Stanley during the previous year, when the functions of the East India Company were transferred to the Crown. Though in some degree restored by his native air, he found his head unequal to any prolonged mental strain. Nevertheless his bearing and conversation, and his grand leonine aspect, seem to have struck the statesmen and officials with whom he had intercourse in England. A man of action—was the title accorded to him by all. During the summer he received the acknowledgments of his countrymen with a quiet modesty which enhanced the esteem universally felt for him. The City of London conferred on him formally, in the Guildhall, the Freedom which had already been bestowed while he was in India. This was one of the two proudest moments in his life. On that occasion he said: "If I was placed in a position of extreme danger and difficulty, I was also fortunate in having around me some of the ablest civil and military officers in India. . . . I have received honours and rewards from my Sovereign. . . . . But I hope that some reward will even yet be extended to those who so nobly shared with me the perils of the struggle." The Universities of Oxford and Cambridge granted him their Honorary Degrees. He was honoured by an invitation to Windsor Castle, and it appears that he must have had several important conversations with the Prince Consort.

On June 24th he received an address signed by eight thousand persons, including Archbishops, Bishops, Members of both Houses of Parliament, Lord Mayors and Mayors, Lord Provosts and Provosts. The national character of this demonstration was thus set forth in a leading-article of the *Times* of the 25th: "Of the names contained in the address hundreds are representative names,—indicating that chiefs of schools and of parties have combined to tender honour to a great man, and that each subscriber was really expressing the sentiments of a considerable body."

The chair was taken on the occasion by the Bishop of London (Archibald Campbell Tait, afterwards Archbishop of Canterbury). Addressing John Lawrence, and recounting the work in the War of the Mutinies, he said:

"When we recollect that at the commencement of the recent mutiny it was not uncommonly said that one cause of our weakness in other parts of India was the necessity which existed of concentrating our forces for the purpose of occupying the Sikh territory; and when we remember on the other hand that through your instrumentality that province which had been our terror became one of the sources of our strength, that instead of concentrating the British forces in the Punjab you were able to send men to aid in the capture of Delhi, so that the weapon which seemed so formidable to our power was by you so wielded as to be our best defence; when we reflect that those very soldiers, who but a few years ago were engaged in mortal conflict with our own, became under your superintendence our faithful allies,—there appears in the whole history something so marvellous that it is but right we should return thanks, not so much to the human instrument, as to God by whom that instrument was employed."

This passage in the Chairman's speech shows an accurate appreciation of the position of the Punjab during the crisis. In the address itself, after due allusion to the war and its results, there comes this special reference to the despatch regarding Christianity in India, which has been already mentioned in a previous chapter.

"You laid down the principle that 'having endeavoured solely to ascertain what is our Christian duty, we should follow it out to the uttermost undeterred by any consideration.' You knew that 'if anything like compulsion enters into our system of diffusing Christianity, the rules of that religion itself are disobeyed, and we shall never be permitted to profit by our disobedience.' You have recorded your conviction that Christian things done in a Christian way will never alienate the heathen. About such things there are qualities which do not provoke distrust nor harden to resistance. It is when unchristian things are done in the name of Christianity, or when Christian things are done in an unchristian way, that mischief and danger are occasioned.' These words are memorable. Their effect will be happy not only on your own age but on ages to come. Your proposal that the Holy Bible should be relieved from the interdict under which it was placed in the Government schools and colleges, was true to the British principle of religious liberty and faithful to your Christian conscience."

Some passages may be quoted as extracts from Lawrence's reply as they are very characteristic. Expressing gratitude for the good opinion of his countrymen, and again commending his officers to the care of their country, he thus proceeds:

"All we did was no more than our duty and even our immediate interest. It was no more than the necessities of our position impelled us to attempt. Our sole chance of escape was to resist to the last. The path of duty, of honour, and of safety was clearly marked out for us. The desperation of our circumstances nerved us to the uttermost. There never, perhaps, was an occasion when it was more necessary to win or to die. To use the words of my heroic brother at Lucknow, it was incumbent on us never to give in. We had no retreat, no scope for compromise. That we were eventually successful against the fearful odds which beset us, was alone the work of the great God who so mercifully vouchsafed His protection."

This passage will probably be regarded as effective oratory, indeed few orators would express these particular points with more of nervous force. Thus an idea may be formed of what his style would have been, had he received training when young, and had he retained his health. But though he had at this time, 1859, frequently to make speeches in public, on all which occasions the modesty, simplicity and straightforwardness of his utterance pleased his hearers, yet he was not at all an orator. In his early and middle life he had never, as previously explained, any practice or need for public speaking. Had he been so practised, he would doubtless have been among speakers, what he actually was among writers, forcible, direct, impressive, not at all ornate or elaborate, perhaps even blunt and brief. In short he would have been an effective speaker for practical purposes, rising on grave occasions even to a rough eloquence—inasmuch as he had self-possession and presence of mind in a perfect degree. But now, as he was fully entered into middle life, all this was impossible by reason of physical depression. Had this depression been anywhere but where it actually was, it might have failed to spoil his public speaking. But its seat was somewhere in the head, and any attempt at impromptu or extempore delivery seemed first to affect the brain, then the voice and even the chest. He could no doubt light up for a moment and utter a few sentences with characteristic fire; or he could make a longer speech quietly to a sympathetic audience; but beyond this he was no longer able to go. As his health improved, his power of speaking increased naturally, still it never became what it might have become had he been himself again physically.

In the autumn of 1859 he proceeds to Ireland, where his wife revisits the scenes of her early years. He returns to London, where he spends a happy Christmas in his domestic circle, with rapidly improving health.

In the spring of 1860, he attests his abiding interest in the cause of religious missions to India by attendance at an important gathering in Exeter Hall, to hear his friend Edwardes (of Peshawur) deliver a remarkable speech.

During the summer months he zealously promotes the holiday amusements of his children. Visitors, calling to see him on public affairs, would find him, not in a library, but in a drawing-room surrounded by his family. In the autumn he visits his birthplace, Richmond in

Yorkshire. Thence he goes to Inverary to be the guest of the Duke and Duchess of Argyll, with both of whom he forms a lasting friendship. Then he receives the Freedom of the City of Glasgow and returns to London.

Early in the following year, 1861, he leaves London and takes a roomy old-fashioned house at Southgate, a few miles to the north of London, where he remains for the remainder of his sojourn in England. To the house is attached some land where he may indulge his taste for farming and his fondness for animals. In the week days he attends the Council of India in London, but his summer evenings he spends at home with his family, and mainly lives a country life.

His position in the Indian Council, where Sir Charles Wood (afterwards Lord Halifax) had succeeded Lord Stanley as Secretary of State for India, was not such as to call his individuality into play. Though he had a voice in the affairs of India, he was no longer a man of action. Even then, however, he impressed his colleagues favourably, and especially the Secretary of State. He felt and expressed great regret at the abolition of the local army of India, and its amalgamation with the army of the Crown. He was not what is termed in England a party man, but he certainly was a moderate Liberal in politics. As a churchman of the Church of England, he was content with his Bible and the Book of Common Prayer.

In 1862 he met Lord Canning, who had resigned his high office as Governor-General, returning home very shortly to die. Then he saw Lord Elgin appointed to fill the important place.

During 1863 he was running the even and quiet

course of his life in England, attending to the work in the Council of India in Whitehall, which for him was not onerous, enjoying rural amusements with his family, playing games with his children, imbibing the country breezes, recovering as much of vigour and nerve as might be possible for a constitution like his which had been sorely tried and severely battered. He became much improved in health, and still more in spirits. He was in easy circumstances, having a salary as member of the Council of India at Whitehall, his annuity for which he had virtually paid by deductions from salary since the date of entering the Civil Service of India, the special pension granted to him by the East India Company, and the moderate competency from his savings during a long service of nearly thirty years. He was himself a man of the simplest tastes and the fewest wants, but he had a large family for whom he was affectionately solicitous. But while liberal and open-handed in every case which called for generosity, he was a thrifty and frugal manager, a good steward in small things of everyday life, even as he had been in national affairs. He nowadays acted on the principle that—

> "The trivial round, the common task,
> Will furnish all we ought to ask;
> Room to deny ourselves; a road
> To bring us daily nearer God."

Thus he did few of the things which men of his repute and position might ordinarily do, and which doubtless he must have often been urged to undertake. He wrote neither books nor brochures, he hardly ever addressed public meetings, he did not preside over learned or philanthropic societies, he took no active part in politics, municipal or national. He sought repose, dignified by the reminiscence of a mighty past. Believing that his life's work was in the main accomplished and his mission ended, he pondered much on the life to come. If there be such things on earth as unclouded happiness and unalloyed contentment, these blessings were his at that time.

But in the autumn of 1863, two events occurred in India to disturb the tenor of his English life. First, a fanatical outbreak occurred among some of the hill tribes near Peshawur, the British arms received a slight check, the excitement spread to some of the neighbouring hills, and seemed likely to extend with rising flames to the various tribes whose fighting power has been set forth in a previous chapter. Next, the Governor-General, Lord Elgin, was stricken with mortal illness and resigned his high office. The choice of the Government at once fell on Lawrence as his successor. That he was the best and fittest man for the arduous place, was manifest as a general reason. But there probably was a particular reason in addition for selecting him, which may have had weight in the minds of the responsible ministers, Lord Palmerston and Sir Charles Wood, namely the incipient danger just mentioned on the Trans-Indus Frontier. A little war might rapidly assume larger proportions; it was essential to preserve India, exhausted by the War of the Mutinies, from further warfare; none would be so competent as he to restrict the area of operations and to speedily finish them. If this additional reason had any operative effect, that was most honourable to him.

So he was on November 30th suddenly offered the post of Governor-General, which he accepted. In the evening he went home and told his wife what had happened, whereupon he met with much of tender remonstrance. As he laughingly said afterwards, it was fortunate that he had accepted that day before going home, for had he gone home first on the understanding that he was to reply the next day, he might have been induced to refuse. He could not but feel, however, some pride and satisfaction, though there were several drawbacks. He was to incur the risk of shortening life, and the certainty of injuring whatever of health might remain to him. He was to be separated from his family just when they most required his attention, and to break up a home which he had established with loving care. He did not at all need advancement, and could hardly add to his fame. But the disinclination which all official men have to decline any important offer, the discipline which renders them anxious to do as they are bid by authority, the disposition which men, long used to arms, feel to don their armour once again —these sentiments constrained him. Though he would no longer seek new duties, yet if they were imposed upon him, it would be his highest pleasure to discharge them well. He had an important interview, before starting, with the Prime Minister, Lord Palmerston. On December 9th, within ten days from receiving the intimation of his appointment, he started from Charing Cross for India, journeying alone, as it was impossible for his wife to leave suddenly the family home.

The continuance to him, while Governor-General of India, of the special pension (given by the late East

India Company as already mentioned in the last chapter) had to be sanctioned by Parliament; and a resolution to this effect was passed by the House of Commons on February 8th, 1864. The terms in which the Secretary of State, Sir Charles Wood, introduced the resolution, and the response received may be quoted from Hansard's *Parliamentary Debates*. He said: "I had no hesitation in recommending Sir John Lawrence to Her Majesty for the Governor-Generalship of India; and within two days from the receipt of the intelligence from India (of Lord Elgin's death) I was authorised to offer the high post to him. He accepted it at once, and knowing the importance of despatch he showed the same zeal for the service of the country which had always distinguished him, by declaring himself ready to leave England for India by the first mail to Calcutta. The services of Sir John Lawrence are so well known and so universally recognised, that it will only be necessary to read the Resolution under which the pension was conferred upon him, passed at a meeting of the Court of Directors (East India Company) on August 11th, 1858—

"'Resolved unanimously that in consideration of the eminent services of Sir John Laird Mair Lawrence, G.C.B., whose prompt, vigorous and judicious measures crushed incipient mutiny in the Punjab and maintained the province in tranquillity during a year of almost universal convulsion, and who by his extraordinary exertions was enabled to equip troops and to prepare munitions of war for distant operations, thus mainly contributing to the recapture of Delhi and to the subsequent successes which attended our arms, and in testimony of the high sense entertained by the East India Company of his public character and conduct throughout a long and distinguished career, an annuity of £2000 be granted to him.'"

From the opposite Bench, Lord Stanley rose and said: "I apprehend that there will be no difference on any side of the House upon this Resolution. I rise merely to express my entire concurrence, having been connected with Indian affairs during part of the time when the services of Sir John Lawrence were performed. This was not a retiring pension, but was a recognition, and a very inadequate recognition, of services as distinguished as had ever been performed by a public servant in India."

The motion was passed by the House of Commons without any dissentient voice, and the manner in which it was received in Parliament, when reported in India, was sure to strengthen John Lawrence's position there.

CHAPTER IX

THE GOVERNMENT OF INDIA

1864-1869

THE work which John Lawrence had heretofore done in India is not of that sort which should be measured statistically. Its material proportions had been indeed considerable, but they were infinitely exceeded by its moral effect. Still some few comparative facts may be noted to show what his new sphere was compared with his old. The Punjab with its dependencies contained, when he left it in 1859, one hundred and forty-five thousand square miles, with twenty-two millions of inhabitants, and paid an annual revenue of two and a half millions sterling. It had been augmented, since its first formation as a British province, by the addition of the Delhi territory. The Indian empire, when he took charge of it in 1864, contained one million three hundred thousand square miles with two hundred and thirty-five millions of inhabitants, paid an annual revenue of fifty-three millions sterling, was defended by an army of nearly two hundred thousand men, including both European and Native troops, and was divided into eleven provincial governments or administrations, under two Governors, three Lieutenant-Governors, three Chief Commissioners, and three Residencies or Governor-General's Agencies.

In January, 1864, Lawrence arrived at Calcutta as Viceroy and Governor-General. He looked much brightened and freshened by a sojourn of four and a half years in England. His old vivacity sparkled again ; he had been softened as well as brightened by his sojourn in England. He walked with a stride, and his seat in the saddle was almost as of yore. His health had been temporarily restored, but had not, as the sequel showed, been re-established.

Usually a new Viceroy and Governor-General is, on landing in India, really new in every sense. The European officers, the Native Princes, Chiefs and people, are strangers to him as he is personally unknown to them. Yet he has great power and wide influence, not only over individuals, but also over large classes and masses, and his personality will for a term of years affect the conduct of the executive and the course of legislation. Consequently when he comes, public expectation is on the tiptoe, and the public gaze is strained to discover what manner of man he may be. It is hard to describe adequately the anxious uncertainty which prevails, and consequently the intensity of the interest which is thus aroused in most instances. But in the instance of Lawrence there was no such novelty. His name was already a household word from one end of the empire to the other. To all men his character, disposition and idiosyncrasy were known by fame, and to numerous individuals, even to many classes, were familiar. Again, other Governors-General arriving in India have been obliged to go to school politically, and almost serve an apprenticeship; but he was already a master workman, and could enter fully and at once upon his whole duty.

As Governor-General he had all the power entrusted to that high functionary by the Acts of Parliament settling the Constitution of British India. As Viceroy he represented the Sovereign on all occasions.

On his arrival at Calcutta he was greeted most cordially by all classes of his countrymen, from the soldiers and sailors upwards. Loud was the chorus of British voices, thick was the concourse of Natives, as the stately vessel, bearing him as its freight, steamed up the broad reaches of the tidal Hooghly, between banks crowned with groves of the cocoa-nut, the palm and the bamboo, approached the forest of masts in the harbour of the Indian capital, and anchored near the ramparts of Fort William, close to the palace of the Governor-General.

Landing in Bengal, he met that section of the Indian population which had but little direct concern in the War of the Mutinies, and was therefore less cognisant of his deeds than the Natives of Northern India; still the Bengalis in their way strove to do him honour. His first levée was one of the most numerously attended levées ever held in Calcutta. He was full of alacrity, and if ever in his life he wore a smiling aspect it was then. Things had heretofore gone well with him in the estimation of all men East and West. The farewell addresses on leaving the Punjab, the addresses of welcome on reaching England, the congratulations at home on his new appointment, the notes of gladness on his return to India, were all present to his mind, and he was breathing the *popularis aura*. Few men, climbing to estate so high as his, have known so little of ungenerous objections or of actual misrepresentation, as he had up to this time.

He was hardly prepared, perhaps, for the fitful moods of public opinion in such a country as India, for the wearing anxieties, the lesser troubles, even the annoyances, to be endured at intervals for some years before the moment when he should lay down the supreme power, and again look back with some pride and satisfaction upon another arduous stage accomplished in life's journey.

He came by the overland route in December at the most favourable season of the year and escaped sea-sickness. As sea life was never quite suitable to his temperament, he did not read nor write much during the voyage, but he must have had time to arrange his thoughts respecting the imperial charge which had been committed to him. As a rule, he meant to deal with matters as they should arise—knowing that these would be numerous, and confident in his own power to dispose of them—rather than to shape out any policy or policies in his mind, or to descry any particular goal which he would strive to reach. Nevertheless he landed in India with certain ideas which might, according to his hope, be realised. As they are quite characteristic of him, some allusion may be here made to them.

During his sojourn in England he had been much impressed with the importance of sanitation or sanitary administration, as likely to become the pressing question of the immediate future. The insanitary condition of Indian cities had affected him in his younger days, and in later years his letters contain allusions to the subject. But something more than spasmodic effort was needed for that rectification which he would now make an imperial concern. To stimulate his recollections he would direct his morning rides to the unhealthiest parts of

Calcutta, and one of his first measures after assuming the general government was to appoint a Sanitary Commission.

But the principle of sanitation had in his mind a special application. He appears while in England to have been conferring with Florence Nightingale regarding military hospitals and the health of the European soldiery. Here, again, as a young man, he had grieved over the intemperance existing among these troops, and partly attributable to injudicious regulations which had been subsequently modified. The War of the Mutinies had brought home to his mind, with greater force than ever, the supreme value of these men to the Eastern empire. He then set himself to observe their barracks, and especially their hospitals, which he used to visit in times of epidemic sickness. He would now use all his might as Governor-General to give them spacious and salubrious barracks, suitable means for recreation, and other resources for the improvement of their condition.

In former years he had witnessed the effects of drought upon districts destitute of artificial irrigation; and it was notorious that drought is the recurring plague not only of the continental climate of Mid-India, as physical geographers term it, but also of the southern peninsula. He had seen the inception of the Ganges canal, the queen of all canals ever undertaken in any age or country; and he would now stimulate the planning and executing of irrigation works great and small.

For this, however, capital was needed, so his financial instinct warned him that the Government of India must cease constructing these necessary works out of revenue—a tardy and precarious process—but must open a capital account for the nation, whereby India might borrow money for reproductive works, on the principle which prevails in all progressive countries.

Lastly, he had while in England reconsidered the principle of what is known as the Permanent Settlement of Bengal, which was much disapproved by the administrative school of his earlier days. He had now come to think that this Settlement possessed much political advantage, in strengthening the basis of landed prosperity, and thus attaching all landowners to the British Government; and so far he was actually prepared to extend it to some other districts beyond Bengal. But he was as keenly alive as ever to its imperfections, as it had neglected the rights of subordinate occupiers. He looked back with thankfulness upon the efforts which had been made in North-western India to preserve these rights. Having some fear that they might in certain circumstances be overridden, he resolved to champion them when necessary. This resolve brought about some trying episodes in his subsequent career.

Thus there were at least five large matters of imperial policy arranged in his mind from the very outset as he set foot once again on the Indian shore. The public sanitation, the physical welfare of the European soldiery, the prevention of famine by irrigation works, the capital account of the national outlay for material improvement, the settlement of agrarian affairs,—these were principles long fixed in his mind. But his conception of them had been widened or elevated by his sojourn in England, and by the fresh influences of political thought there.

From the beginning of January to the middle of April

he worked, with his Executive Council, at Government House in Calcutta. The Councillors were five in number for the several departments, Foreign, Home, Legislative, Public Works, Financial, Revenue, Military; and in addition the Commander-in-Chief of the army. In ordinary matters the decision of the Government was formed by a majority of votes; but in matters of public safety he had power to act on his own authority alone. He was able to maintain excellent relations with his colleagues in Council. The Foreign Department was ordinarily kept in his own hands. He worked from six o'clock in the morning till five in the evening daily, despatching current business in all departments with amazing promptitude and completeness withal. He issued the necessary orders on the speedy and successful termination of the military operations on the Trans-Indus Frontier, which have been already mentioned. He reviewed Volunteers, founded a Sailors' Home, inspected sanitation in the Native city, and made the acquaintance of all important persons of every nationality in the capital. His health stood the new test fairly well, but he suffered at times from headache. In the middle of April he started for Simla, taking his Council with him. On his way thither he revisited the Asylum for the orphan children of European soldiers at the Himalayan station of Kassowli, founded with much private munificence by his brother Henry. He had not seen this beautiful Simla since he met Lord Dalhousie there in 1851. Though he said little, he pondered much on all that had happened to him and his since then, the perils escaped, the victories won.

After his arrival at Simla having reviewed his own

position and prospects, he wrote to Sir Charles Wood, the Secretary of State in London, on this subject. He said explicitly that he found himself unable to work all the year round at Calcutta, and especially in the hot and unhealthy season there; that if he were allowed to spend the summer months in the Himalayas, he could retain his post; otherwise he wished to resign in the spring of the following year and return to England. By Sir Charles Wood's reply he was requested to stay in office, with the understanding that he might reside wherever he chose within the Himalayas or other hill-regions of India. Regarding his Council the reply was not quite so clear, but in the end it was virtually conceded that he might exercise his own discretion in taking his colleagues with him. At all events he determined to stay for four out of his five allotted years in India, and arranged that his wife should join him at Calcutta by the end of the year 1864.

He soon decided that during his tenure of office the Government of India shall, barring unforeseen events, spend the summer months at Simla, that is the Governor-General, the Executive Council, a part of the Legislative Council, and the principal Secretaries. He would not separate himself from them: he did not wish to have them acting at headquarters in many cases without him; nor did he desire to act in some cases alone without them. He thought it better that, with the growing increase of business, they should be all together.

At that time it was the fashion to propose various situations in the empire, one in the south another in the west and so on, for the permanent capital and headquarters of the Government of India, involving the abandonment of Calcutta for this purpose; but he objected to all such schemes, considering them to be crude. In the first place, such a move would be inordinately expensive; in the second, Calcutta was, he thought, the best of all available positions. Though it is actually a sea-port, yet its position is by nature rendered unassailable by an attack from the sea; its trade places it in the first rank of mercantile cities; the districts around it are wealthy, fertile, populous and peaceful; these advantages he duly appreciated. During the disturbances of 1857 he remembered that Lower Bengal around Calcutta was undisturbed, and paid its tens of millions of rupees into the State Treasury, and that while half the empire was convulsed, order was preserved at the imperial centre. Thus he would hold fast to Calcutta and settle his Government there, at least during the cool season of each year when trade and industry are in their fullest activity.

But he would have his Government sojourn during the hot weather of each year in the refreshing climate of the Himalayas. He had no hesitation in choosing Simla for this purpose, as being the only mountain station that could furnish house-accommodation for the influx of sojourners; as being easily accessible by rail and road at all seasons; as having politically a good position sufficiently near the North-western Frontier, yet not so near as to be within reach of danger; and as being immediately surrounded by a peaceful population. He was sensible of the natural beauty, the varied charms, the salubrious climate of the place, and his choice has been fully ratified by the Governors-General who have succeeded him.

His Government, while sojourning at Simla, would transact all its administrative business for the time, and proceed with some parts of its legislation. But he would reserve for its residence at Calcutta all those bills or projects of law which might be of general importance, and wherein contact with public opinion might be specially desirable.

He was now by the autumn of 1864, fairly launched on his career as Viceroy and Governor-General. His health had been slightly shaken by the change from England to Calcutta, of which the climate agreed with him less than that of any other place in India. But it soon revived in the Himalayan air. He kept up his early riding in the morning while at Calcutta, but was induced by the pressure of business to intermit it at Simla. However he took exercise in the afternoon fully, and so during this year and 1865 he remained fairly well; indeed during the summer of 1865 he was better than he had been for many years, that is since his Trans-Sutlej days. But he was not so well in 1866, and in the summer of 1867 he intimated to the Secretary of State, who was then Sir Stafford Northcote, that he might have to retire early in 1868 having completed his four years. The Secretary of State, however, on public grounds requested him to remain till the end of his five years if possible, that is till the beginning of 1869. So he braced his determination to remain his allotted term. He said in private that it would be a great satisfaction to him to serve out his time, and to hand over the work to his successor without any arrears. From 1867, however, he became weaker physically by slow, perhaps by imperceptible degrees, and that general condition naturally set up lesser ailments from time to time; while the clear brain and the unconquerable will remained.

Apprehensions of ill health, however, were not the only reason why he thought in 1867 of resigning office. He was indeed as good, efficient and successful a Viceroy and Governor-General as India ever had; still the course of affairs did not exactly suit his masterful genius. Grand events would have afforded scope for the mighty capacity he was conscious of possessing. The country was for the most part at peace, nevertheless he was troubled even harassed by divers incidents which affected the public interests. The empire was making steady progress under his care and recovering its stability after a severe convulsion; yet mishaps, reverses, plagues of all sorts, would occur through no fault of his. But he would not relieve himself of responsibility for what might be amiss or go wrong in any part of his vast charge, and often he was tempted to exclaim,

> "The time is out of joint, oh! cursed spite
> That I was ever born to set it right!"

Hitherto the *popularis aura* had been with him; he had not yet felt that chilling blast of unpopularity which sooner or later never fails to overtake public men of mark and vigour such as his. No man had known less than he the carping, the cavilling, the captiousness of critics, or the misrepresentation of opponents. He had never swam with the stream, but rather had cut out a channel for the stream and made it flow with him. Thus the wear and tear of his former life had arisen from notable causes, but not from the friction of an adverse current. Now, however, he was to taste of all these small adversities. He was indeed to rule an empire thoroughly well in ordinary times, and to suffer the vexations which ordinarily beset rulers and make their heads "lie uneasy." He strove manfully to hide his sensitiveness when attacked or impugned; for all that, he was more sensitive to these attacks than he need have been, in regard to their intrinsic deserts. The deference, the cordiality, even the affection (as he himself gratefully described it) of the reception which greeted him in England, and which was repeated on his first landing in India, had scarcely prepared him for the provocations, petty indeed but yet sharp, which awaited him in the subsequent years. As a man of action he had been used to arguments of an acute even fierce character, yet they were short and decisive either for or against him. But now he had to work his government through an Executive Council of some six members, in which the discussions were partly on paper daily, and partly by word of mouth at weekly meetings. The paper-controversies he could bear; if he had a majority on his side the decision would be couched in a few of his pithy sentences and no more was heard of it. But at times the weekly debates tried him sorely; he listened like patience on a monument, but he sighed inwardly. India being unavoidably a land of personal changes, the composition of his Council varied from year to year with outgoing and incoming men. In the nature of things it was inevitable that some of his colleagues should support him more and others less, while some opposed. He rejoiced in the hearty aid afforded by some, and grieved over the opposition, or as it appeared to him the thwarting, counteracting conduct of others, which was different from anything that he had previously endured. Again, he thankfully acknowledged in the end the support he received from successive Secretaries of State in England, and certainly the Government in England sincerely desired to sustain his authority; but meanwhile cases occurred wherein he considered himself insufficiently supported from home, and one case where even his old friends in the Council of India in Whitehall counteracted his wishes. Respecting the action of Secretaries of State he hardly made sufficient allowance for Parliamentary difficulties, which prevent the men who are nominally in power from being their own masters. It has been acutely remarked of him that he was not versatile; in truth versatility in the face of opposition was not among his qualities. He hardly possessed that peculiar resourcefulness (for which, for instance, the great Warren Hastings was distinguished) whereby one expedient having failed or one way being stopped, another is found, perhaps circuitously, the goal being all the while kept in view. Being human he must needs have faults, though the proportion which these bore to his virtues was small indeed; he certainly had a tendency to chafe over-much, yet if this be a fault, then owing to his self-command, it affected himself only but not others. He loved power, indeed, which he habitually described in a favourite Persian phrase as *khûd-raftâri*, which is an elegant synonym for having one's own way. Such power was, in his estimation, to be wielded not capriciously but under the constraint of a well-informed conscience. He had scarcely thought out the fact, however, that in few modern nations, and least of all in the British, can there be such a thing strictly speaking as power, though there may be powerful influence. For the jealously-watched and tightly-bound "thing which is mocked by the name of power," he had scant appreciation. In short, his position presented much that was novel rather than pleasant, though he encountered less of novelty than any Governor-General who had preceded him. But it is well in passing to sketch these lesser traits, for the portraiture of the real man in all his greatness and goodness.

To give an account of his Government at large, would be to write the history of an empire during five years, and space cannot here be afforded for such a task. Again, to do justice to all the coadjutors who helped him, would be to set forth at least parts of the careers of many eminent men, and that, too, is beyond the limits of this work. All that is possible, then, is to analyse or sum up briefly the main heads of his policy and achievements, with the proviso that, what for the sake of brevity is attributed to him nominally, is really attributable to him with the Councils, both Executive and Legislative, the extensive Secretariat, the Presidencies, and the provincial Governors or Administrators. These heads may be arranged in the following order:—the army, the works of material improvement, the sanitation, the finances, the landed settlement, the legislation, the public service, the national education, the state ceremonies, the foreign policy; and to each of them, as respecting him particularly, a short notice will be afforded.

In the military branch, he had not much to do with the reorganisation of the army for India. That had been done during the interval since his departure from India in 1859. Some changes had been made, against which he had protested from his place in Council at Whitehall, but now he had loyally to accept the accomplished facts, and to make the changes work well through good management. Keeping his eye ever fixed on the national finance, he rejoiced to find the Native Army reduced in numbers, and the overgrown levies (which had been raised during the War of the Mutinies) now disbanded throughout the country or transferred to the newly-organised Police. The strength of the European troops varied from seventy to seventy-five thousand men: which was, in his judgment, the minimum compatible with safety in time of peace. He never forgot what his Native advisers used to drop into his ear during the Mutiny—namely this, that in India the European soldier is the root of our power. Knowing how hard it would be for the English Government to provide, and for the Indian Government to bear, the cost of a larger number, he bent himself to make the European soldiery as effective as possible by improving their life and lot in the East. Everything that pertained to their health, recreation, comfort, enlightenment, employment in leisure time, and general welfare, moral or physical, he steadfastly supported. At the basis of all these improvements lay the question of constructing new barracks or reconstructing old buildings, on reformed principles sanitary as well as architectural; and for this he was prepared to incur an outlay of several millions sterling. Protracted discussions ensued in his Executive Council in regard to the situations for the new barracks, causing delay which distressed him. He insisted that the buildings should be placed in those centres of population, and those strategic points, where old experience had shown that the presence of European soldiers was necessary. So after a while the work of barrack-building went on to his satisfaction. Criticism, even objections, were soon levelled against these operations, and the barracks were styled "palatial," under the notion that they were extravagantly good; but he was not thereby at all turned from his purpose.

In active warfare operations were undertaken near the Trans-Indus Frontier on two occasions; the first of these, which has already been mentioned at the moment of his arrival in India, was known by the name of Umbeyla, the second was remembered as that of the Black Mountain. Otherwise he thankfully observed the pacification of that difficult Frontier, which had successfully been effected by the policy of himself and his brother from 1849 onwards, as set forth in a previous chapter. One little war, indeed, he had which was from first to last hateful to him, but which he turned to excellent account for British interests, as the event has subsequently proved; this is known to history as the Bhûtan campaign. On his arrival he found that a mission had been already despatched to that semi-barbarous principality in the eastern Himalayas over-looking Bengal, and that the British envoy had been insulted and even maltreated. Redress was demanded, and this being refused, he had resort to arms; and during the course of these operations in a wild, wooded, malarious and mountainous country, a small British force in a hill-fort was cut off from its water-supply by the enemy's devices, and had to beat a somewhat disastrous retreat. The disaster was soon retrieved by the recapture of the place, and full preparations were made for a decisive advance when the enemy sued for terms; whereon he laid down the British conditions of peace. These being accepted, he was glad to save the lives of a miserable foe from destruction, and the British troops from inglorious warfare in an unhealthy country. The main point in the conditions on which he concluded peace was the cession by Bhûtan to the British of a rich sub-Himalayan tract called the Dûars, on his agreeing to pay a certain sum annually to the Bhûtanese. He felt the value of this tract to the British, as was indeed manifest then, and has been proved by subsequent experience. He knew that the payment of this small subsidy would just preserve the Bhûtanese from that pecuniary desperation which leads to border incursions, and would give us a hold on them, as it could be withheld in event of their misconduct in future; and in fact they have behaved well ever since. But the terms were by the European community at Calcutta deemed inadequate and derogatory after all that had happened; and he was subjected to much severe criticism, which however did not move, though it doubtless grieved, him at this stage of his career.

He rejoïced in the opportunity afforded by the expedition to Abyssinia for helping his old friend Napier to collect an effective force from India, to be equipped for very active service and to be despatched from the Presidency of Bombay.

In respect to material improvement, he pressed onwards the construction of railways and canals. There had been by no means an entire, but only a partial, suspension of these works during the War of the Mutinies, and the period of disturbance which followed; but now as peace reigned throughout the land, he prosecuted these beneficent operations with more energy than ever, and at no previous time in Indian history had progress been so systematised as now. This could only be done by establishing a capital account for the State, according to the principle which, as already mentioned, had been working in his mind when he recently landed in India. The cost of these works having heretofore been defrayed from current revenue, their progress had been precarious, but he would place their finance on a sure basis by treating the expenditure as capital outlay and raising loans for that purpose. The interest on these would be defrayed from current revenue, as he would have no such thing as paying interest out of capital. For the due calculation of the demand to be made on the money-market for the loans, he caused a forecast to be made of the canals and railways recommended for construction during a cycle of years. He proposed that the future railways should be constructed not by private companies with guarantee by the State of interest on outlay, but by the State itself. With a view to lessening the capital outlay in future, he leaned towards the introduction of a narrower gauge than that heretofore in use. The introduction of the capital account into Indian finance has not only stimulated, but also regulated and ensured the material development of the empire; and this is a prominent feature in his administration.

Besides the ordinary arguments for accelerating the construction of railways, there was the necessity of perfecting our military communications, in order to obtain a tighter grasp of the country than heretofore. The lesson of 1857-8 had taught him how much this hold had needed strengthening. Again, beyond the usual reasons for excavating canals of irrigation for agriculture in a thirsty land, he felt the obligation to protect the people from the consequences of drought. No warning, indeed, was required by him in this behalf, otherwise it would have been furnished by the experience of the Orissa famine in 1866-7. In that somewhat inaccessible province the drought occurred one year and the people bore it, but it continued during the second and even the third year, reducing their straitened resources to starvation point; then towards the end of the third year heavy downpours of rain caused inundation to submerge the remnant of the crops; thus, in his own expressive words, "that which the drought spared the floods drowned." He had been very uneasy about the prospect of the famine, but the province was under the Government of Bengal subject to the control of the Governor-General, and he was bound to consult the local authorities. He accepted for the moment the assurance of the Lieutenant-Governor of Bengal, who had proceeded to the spot to make personal inquiries, to the effect that the precautions taken to prevent mortality from famine were sufficient. Still he remained anxious till further tidings came, and these were bad. Then he caused the most strenuous efforts to be put forth but they were too late to save life, and their efficacy was impaired by a still further misfortune, because contrary gales kept grain-laden ships tossing about within sight of the shore and unable to land their cargoes. Though he was not to blame in all the circumstances, still this disaster cut him to the quick, and he fretted at the thought of what might have been done to save life had he himself been wielding the executive powers locally as in former days, instead of exercising only a general control as Governor-General. The loss being irreparable, all he could now do was to make the strictest inquisition regarding the failure in foresight which delayed the relief in the first instance, to take additional precautions by the light of this melancholy experience, and so to prevent the possibility of its recurrence. Thus under him from that time a new era of development, and especially of canal-making arose happily for Orissa.

For sanitation, he acted on the view which had opened out before him on his way from England for India. The Sanitary Commission appointed by him made searching inquiries and followed these up with suggestions professional or practical. He sanctioned expenditure by Government on drainage, water-supply, open spaces, and the like, in the stations or around the buildings which belonged to the State. In all the places which were made under municipal institutions he encouraged the local corporations to do the same. Through his precept or example a fresh impulse was given to these beneficent works at every capital city, industrial centre, or considerable town, throughout the Bengal Presidency—more than half the empire—and a general quickening of municipal life was the consequence. His influence could not under the constitution of British India be equally direct in the Madras and Bombay Presidencies but there also it was felt as a practical encouragement. Thus though he may not be called the originator of Indian Sanitation, yet he was the founder of it on a systematic basis, and he established it as a department of the State administration.

The finances caused him trouble from the first even to the last day of his incumbency. The scheme for housing and lodging the European army in India, according to humane and civilised plans, was to cost ten millions sterling (for, say, seventy-five thousand men), and out of that he caused five millions to be spent during his five years of office. He was most unwilling to borrow for this purpose, holding firmly that the charge must be defrayed from current revenues, and so it was. But then it caused some difficulty in the finances, and he had to devise additional means for making the income balance the expenses. Always having a heart for the poor, and believing that their resources were not at all elastic, he was resolved to avoid taxing the masses of the population any further. On the other hand he thought that the rich escaped paying their full share. So he proposed to renew the income tax, which had been introduced in 1860 by James Wilson (the economist and financier sent out from England) and remitted in 1862. He was unable to obtain, however, the necessary concurrence of his Council. Then he reluctantly consented to a proposal of the Council that duties should be imposed on certain articles of export which, in the economic circumstances of the moment, were able to bear the impost. The ordinary objection to export-duties was urged in England and even in Parliament, so these were disallowed by the Secretary of State; and thus he suffered a double annoyance. His own proposal had been refused by his Council, and their proposal, to which he agreed as a choice of evils, had been rejected by the Secretary of State. The following year he induced his Council to accept a modified income-tax, under the name of a License-Tax. This was, he knew, inferior to a scientific income-tax, inasmuch as it failed in touching all the rich; still it did touch the well-to-do middle class, heretofore almost exempt from taxation, and that was something. This plan was passed into law by the Legislative Council at Calcutta, but the passage met with embittered opposition from outside in the European as well as in the Native Community; he stood firm, however, and this time was supported both by his Council in India and by the Secretary of State in England. But he knew that this measure, though much better than nothing, was insufficient, and he ceased not from urging the imposition of the income-tax proper. Indeed during his fifth and last year he laid the foundation and prepared the way for that tax, which was actually imposed after his departure, and which during several succeeding years saved the finances from ultimate deficit.

During his five years, however, there were five and a quarter millions sterling of deficit, and two and three quarter millions of surplus, leaving a net deficit of two and a half millions. This deficit was, indeed, more than accounted for by the expenses of five millions on the barracks; but it would never have occurred, had he been properly supported in the sound fiscal measures proposed by him. The financial result in the end, though fully capable of explanation, did indeed fall short of complete success; but this partial failure did not at all arise from any fault of his. Indeed it occurred despite his well-directed exertions. He left India with somewhat gloomy anticipations regarding its financial future. He feared lest his countrymen should fail to appreciate the standing difficulty of Indian finance. He knew that the Natives may have more means relatively to their simple wants than the corresponding classes in European countries, and in that sense may not be poor. But he thought that their power of paying revenue down in cash was very small according to a European standard, and that their fiscal resources were singularly inelastic.

In connection with finance he was much troubled by the failure of the Bank of Bombay. On his arrival in India the American Civil War, then at its height, was causing a rapid rise in the value of cotton in Western India, and an excessive speculation in consequence. On the cessation of the war in 1865 he saw this speculation collapse, and became anxious for the fate of the Bank of Bombay which was a State institution. He did his utmost to guide and assist the Government of Bombay in preventing a catastrophe. But despite his efforts the Bank fell, and its fall was keenly discussed in England generally and in the House of Commons. Then a commission of inquiry was appointed, which after complete investigation remarked upon the steadiness and carefulness displayed by him at least, while it distributed blame among several authorities.

Much was done in his time, more than ever before, for legislation. He took a lively interest in the proceedings of the Legislative Council for India; it consisted of some thirteen members, of whom six belonged to the Executive Council, and seven, partly official and partly non-official, were nominated by the Governor-General; and it was apart from the local legislatures of Bengal, Madras, and Bombay. He assiduously presided over its deliberations, which at that time embraced such important matters as civil and criminal procedure, transfer of property, contract, evidence, negotiable securities, and others. During no period of Indian history has legislation of a fundamental, and, so to speak, scientific character been more remarkably advanced than during his incumbency of five years. He was throughout assisted by English Jurists in England, and in India especially.

In one legislative measure he was able to take a strong part personally, and that was the Punjab Tenancy Act. It appeared to him that in various ways the rights secured (by the land settlement in that Province as already mentioned) to certain classes of cultivators, as separate from peasant proprietors, were being gravely threatened. So he procured the passing of a law for the preservation of the rights and interests in these numerous tenancies under legal definitions.

Cognate to this subject, a question arose in Oude regarding tenant-right, in which he acted with decisive effect. While anxious that the landed aristocracy (styled the Talukdars) in this Province should be maintained in the position ultimately guaranteed to them by Lord Canning in 1859, he was equally resolved that the subordinate rights of occupants and cultivators should be protected. He, in common with others, believed that their rights had been secured simultaneously with those of the Talukdars. But during the subsequent five years this security had, he found, been disturbed, and further measures were needed for protection. He therefore caused these tenant-rights or occupancy tenures to be protected by additional safeguards, which have since been embodied in legislative enactments. These measures of his aroused keen opposition in Northern and North-eastern India, and especially in Calcutta, as the landlord interest in Bengal made common cause with the Talukdars of Oude. Thus much invective was levelled at him by the Anglo-Indian newspaper-press. Then the agitation began to spread from India to England: the influential few could make their cry heard across the seas, the voiceless million could not; that was all the greater reason why he would take care of the million. He held that the question was one of justice or injustice towards a deserving and industrious class of British subjects. His mind, however, was exercised by this controversy in India mainly because he apprehended that the ground of argumentative battle might be shifted to England, and perhaps even to the floor of the House of Commons. Though he fully hoped that the then Secretary of State, Sir Charles Wood, and the Cabinet would support him, yet he was prepared, indeed almost determined, to give up his high office if his policy in Oude should fail to be sustained. He used to say to his intimate friends at the time that he would stand or resign upon his policy in Oude. This is borne out by a letter of his to Sir Charles Wood which has since been published by his biographer, and from which a characteristic passage may be quoted.

"What could make me take the course I have done in favour of the Ryots of Oude, but a strong sense of duty? I understand the question right well, as indeed must every man who has had anything to do with settlement-work. I have no wish to harm the Talukdars. On the contrary, I desire to see fair-play to their interests. . . . It would be a suicidal act for me to come forward and modify the instructions given recently. The Home Government may do this. Parliament may say what it thinks proper. But, of my own free will, I will not move, knowing as I do, that I am right in the course which has been adopted. Did ever any one hear of the Government of India learning that a class of men were not having fair-play at the time of settlement, and then failing to interfere or to issue such orders as the case appeared to demand?"

In the sequel he was generously sustained by the Government in England, and the retrospect of this episode was pleasant to him as he believed it to be a victory for justice.

In respect to the public service in its several branches, it fell to his lot to recommend, and obtain sanction from the Government in England for, some beneficent measures. A revision of the rules regarding leave in India and furlough to Europe, for the three great classes of Government, namely, the Indian Army, the Covenanted Civil Service, and the Uncovenanted Service, had been pending for some time before his arrival. Knowing well the bearings of this many-sided question, he resolved to settle it in a manner befitting the merits of the public servants whose labours and efforts he had witnessed in so many fields of action. He accordingly appointed the most competent persons in India to frame suitable sets of rules, which he induced the Government in England to sanction with but slight modifications.

The simple record of this great fact affords no idea of the attention he personally gave to the multiform and often complex details which involved many conflicting considerations. The rules were demanded by the requirements of the age, and would sooner or later have been passed, at least in their essentials, whoever had been Governor-General; but it is to his sympathy, his trained intelligence, his knowledge and experience, that these great branches of the public service owe the speedy concession, in so acceptable a manner, of the boons which those rules bestow.

Respecting the national education, he allowed the Universities, which had been already established at Calcutta, Madras, and Bombay, to work out their own views. It was in regard to elementary education and village schools that he chiefly interested himself, and with considerable effect. He also helped the Bishop of Calcutta to establish schools at Himalayan stations for European and East Indian children. The progress of religious missions, belonging to all denominations of Christians, afforded him the liveliest satisfaction. He foresaw the possibility of converting large numbers among tribes that had not yet fallen under any of the dominant religions of the East. The example set by the lives of the missionaries produced, in his judgment, a good effect politically by raising the national repute of British people in the eyes of the Natives. Though he was guarded and discreet in his public utterances and in his official conduct, yet his private munificence was always flowing in this direction. When at Calcutta in the winter, he would spend the later part of his afternoons in visiting Christian schools and institutions. He gave a never-failing support to the clergy and all ministers of religion in the discharge of their sacred functions, and became a rallying point around which all influences for good might gather.

A farewell address was voted to him at a conference of missionaries at Calcutta, which comprised a remarkable list of measures attributed by them to his influence. These measures of his, which these competent observers selected for mention, were of a prosaic and unambitious description. But thereby was evinced his insight into the wants of the very humblest and least in the Native population, and his anxiety to render British rule acceptable to his Indian fellow-subjects.

At the same time an address from the Bishop and clergy acknowledged his efforts for the moral and spiritual advancement of the European soldiery, and the effect of his example in promoting true religion among our fellow-countrymen.

To the hospitalities and social ceremonies, becoming to the position of Viceroy, he paid due attention, as was proper in a country where external style is much considered. But he had no longer the buoyancy for entering joyously into social intercourse on a large scale. Regarding the ceremonies of the stateliest character, organised specially for the Native princes and chiefs, he was very particular. These levées or assemblages, called Durbars, signifying a concourse of eminent personages from great distances and requiring long preparation, can only be held on rare occasions, and under all Governors-General have been historically memorable; he held three such during his incumbency, at Lahore, at Agra, and at Lucknow.

The Durbar at Lahore was wondrous even among these occasions which have all excited wonder. The princes, the chiefs, the feudatories of the empire, from the Punjab, the Himalayas, the Trans-Indus frontier, and even from Afghanistan, vied with each other in doing honour to the man who in their eyes was the embodiment of British might, and had returned as the Queen's representative to the centre-point of his labours and the scene of his former triumphs. This moment was the second of the two proudest moments of his life, the first having been that at the Guildhall in London. He found his bosom friend, Sir Robert Montgomery (to whom he had made over charge of the Punjab when departing for England in 1859), still in the position of Lieutenant-Governor. The manner in which his services were remembered by his old associates, is shown by the following passage from the Lieutenant-Governor's speech, which was applauded with rapture: "Then came 1857. The Punjab under his grasp stood firm. Delhi must be regained or India lost. The Punjab was cut off from all aid. It poured down at his bidding from its hills and plains the flower of the native chivalry. The city was captured and we were saved. We are here to welcome him this day, in a hall erected to his memory by his Punjab friends."

His Durbar was held in a beautiful plain lying between the castellated city of Lahore and the river Râvi, which became for the nonce a tented field. Moving to his place there, he looked around at the noble mosque turned by the Sikhs into a magazine, but lately restored to the Moslems by the British—at the palace of the Mogul emperors—at the tombof Runjeet Sing, the Lion-king of the Punjab—and further off across the river, at the still nobler mausoleum of the emperor Jehangir. Amidst these historic surroundings he addressed to the assembly a speech in the vernacular of Hindostan, probably the first speech that had ever been made by a Viceroy in this language. The whole of his well-considered oration is worth reproduction; but the quoting of one passage only must suffice.

"I recognise the sons of my old allies, the Maharaja of Cashmere and Puttiala; the Sikh chiefs of Malwa and the Manjha; the Rajpût chiefs of the hills; the Mahommedan Mulliks of Peshawur and Kohat; the Sirdars of the Derajat, of Hazara, and of Delhi. All have gathered together to do honour to their old ruler. My friends! Let me tell you of the great interest which the illustrious Queen of England takes in all matters connected with the welfare, comfort and contentment of the people of India. Let me inform you, when I returned to my native country, and had the honour of standing in the presence of Her Majesty, how kindly she asked after the welfare of her subjects in the East. Let me tell you, when that great Queen appointed me her Viceroy of India, how warmly she enjoined on me the duty of caring for your interests. Prince Albert, the Consort of Her Majesty, the fame of whose greatness and goodness has spread through the whole world, was well acquainted with all connected with this country, and always evinced an ardent desire to see its people happy and flourishing."

His next Durbar was at Agra, again in a tented plain near the river Jumna, almost within sight of the peerless Taj Mahal, with its gleaming marble, the acknowledged gem of all the architecture in the world, and not far from the red-stone fortress of Akbar the Great. Hither he had summoned the princes and chiefs of two great divisions of the empire which are still almost entirely under Native administration. He utilises the pomp and magnificence with which he is surrounded, in order to give weight and solemnity to his exhortation. Again he delivers to the assembly a speech in the language of Hindostan, which really forms an imperial lecture to Oriental rulers on the duty of ruling well, and is probably the most noteworthy utterance of this description that ever proceeded from British lips. Every sentence, almost every word, of his oration was adapted to a Native audience. Without any vain compliments he reminds them of their besetting faults, and declares to them, "that peace and that security from outward violence which the British Government confers on your territories, you must each of you extend to your people." He admonishes them, in tones bland and dignified but still earnest and impressive, to improve their roads for traffic, their schools for the young, their hospitals for the sick, their police for repressing crime, their finances. He urges them to enlighten their minds by travelling beyond their own dominions. Knowing their passion for posthumous fame and their leaning towards flattery, he takes advantage of these sentiments thus,

> "It has often happened after a chief has passed away that he has not been remembered as a good ruler. Great men while living often receive praise for virtues which they do not possess; and it is only after this life is ended that the real truth is told. The names of conquerors are forgotten. But those of virtuous chiefs live for ever."

Then in order to add encouragement, after impressive advice, he proceeds thus—in reference to their disputes among themselves regarding precedence—

"The British Government will honour that chief most who excels in the management of his people, and does most for the improvement of his country. There are chiefs in this Durbar who have acquired a reputation in this way—I may mention the Maharaja Scindia and the Bêgum of Bhopal. The death of the late Nawab Ghour Khan of Jowrah was a cause of grief to me, for I have heard that he was a wise and beneficent ruler. The Raja of Sîtamow in Malwa is now ninety years old, and yet it is said that he manages his country very well. The Raja of Ketra in Jeyepore has been publicly honoured for the wise arrangements he has made in his lands."

His third and last Durbar was at Lucknow, after the controversy (already mentioned) with the Talukdars had been happily settled. They found that the compromise on which he insisted for the protection of their tenants, was quite workable, that it left a suitable margin for the landlords, and that with its acceptance the thorough support of the British Government to their Talukdâri status would be secured. So they in their turn emulated their brethren of other provinces in doing him honour. Mounted on seven hundred elephants in a superb procession, they rode with him into Lucknow past the ruins (carefully preserved) of the hastily formed defences, and of the battered Residency where his brother Henry had been mortally wounded. The city of Lucknow is artistically not so fine as Lahore and Agra, the scenes of the two former Durbars; still he is greeted by a fair spectacle, as the city stands with a long perspective of cupolas, towers and minarets on the bank of the Goomti. The aspect of Lucknow has never been better described than by the greatest man who ever ruled there, his brother Henry, who wrote:

"The modern city of Lucknow is both curious and splendid. There is a strange dash of European architecture among its Oriental buildings. Travellers have compared the place to Moscow and Constantinople, and we can easily fancy the resemblance: gilded domes surmounted by the crescent; tall slender pillars and lofty colonnades; houses that look as if they had been transplanted from Regent Street; iron railings and balustrades; cages some containing wild beasts, others filled with strange bright birds; gardens, fountains, and litters, and English barouches."

Again there comes the gorgeous assemblage in the tented field with the speech in Hindostani from his dais as Viceroy, and the last of these dramatic occasions is over. Believing this to be his final utterance in public Durbar, he throws a parting solemnity into his language. After acknowledging the address just presented by the Talukdars, whereby they admit the considerateness towards them, as superior land-owners, with which the rights of the subordinate proprietor and tenancy-holders had been defined—he speaks to them thus: "Talukdars! Though we differ in race, in religion, in habits of thought, we are all created by the same God; we are all bound by the same general laws; and we shall all have to give an account to Him at the last of the manner in which we have obeyed His commandments. In this way there is a common bond of union among us all, whether high or low, rich or poor, learned or ignorant."

While at Lucknow he visited his brother Henry's lowly tomb, the room where the mortal wound from a bursting shell had been inflicted, and the remains of the defences which had been hastily thrown up in that emergency He must at the moment have conjured up the thoughts to which the poet has given expression:

"Frail were the works that defended the hold that we held
with our lives;
Death in our innermost chamber, and death at our slight
barricade;
'Never surrender, I charge you; but every man die at his
post!'—
Voice of the dead whom we loved, our Lawrence the best
of the brave."

These ceremonial occasions can give no idea of the business-like attention which he gave to the affairs of the numerous Native States of the Indian Empire. He remembered thankfully the signal services which they (with the fewest exceptions) had rendered during the disturbances of 1857-58. In his judgment their existence was advantageous to British interests in India, as forming a safety-valve to release discontent of several kinds, which otherwise might be pent up till it burst forth injuriously. He believed that they afford a field of employment to many who cannot find any adequate scope in the British territories, and that hereby a nucleus of influence is constituted in favour of a strong imperial Paramount.

The only part of his policy remaining to be summarised is that relating to foreign affairs, which mainly concern Afghanistan. It has been shown in a previous chapter that originally he desired to avoid having anything to do with Afghanistan, but that under the directions of two Governors-General in those days, he had negotiated two treaties with the Afghan Amir Dost Mahommed, involving the regular payment of pecuniary subsidies. When he himself became Governor-General, he saw Afghanistan torn by internecine and fratricidal contests after the death of Dost Mahommed. He scrupulously stood aloof from these civil wars, espousing neither party in any contest, willing to recognise the man who should establish himself as *de facto* ruler, but waiting till such establishment should be complete before according formal recognition. At length he was able to recognise officially Shir Ali, who had practically fought his way to the status of Amir, on the understanding that the periodical subsidy would follow as a consequence.

But having confirmed friendly relations with the Amir of the day by substantial gifts and by moral support, he planted his foot, so to speak, on this line as on a limit not to be passed. He considered that the Amir when subsidised and otherwise well treated by us, ought to be the friend of our friends and the enemy of our enemies. Otherwise he would scrupulously respect the Amir's independence as ruler of Afghanistan. On the other hand, he would have on the British side no offensive and defensive alliance with the Amir, lest the British Government should be drawn into complications owing to errors on the Afghan side. If this principle should seem one-sided, it was, he held, unavoidable in the circumstances. But he would let the Amir, when in the right, feel sure of British support, provided always that Britain were not expected to send troops into Afghanistan. He set his face not only against any interference in affairs within Afghanistan, but also against the despatch of British officers to Caubul, Candahar or anywhere else. He deemed that the presence of British officers in Afghanistan would spoil everything, would kindle fanatical jealousy, and would end in their own murder.

The Afghans, he was convinced, will be the enemies of those who interfere, and the friends of those who protect them from such interference. Therefore, as he would say in effect, let us leave Russia (our natural opponent) to assume, if she dares, the part of interference, and let the British adopt the attitude of protection; that would be the only chance of obtaining an Afghan alliance in British interests. In that case he hoped that the Afghans would offer a deadly opposition to a Russian advance towards India through their inhospitable country. Even then he hoped only, without feeling sure, for the conduct of the Afghans cannot be foreseen. They might, he would often say, be tempted to join the Russians on the promise of sharing in the plunder of India; but such junction would not be probable: on the other hand, if the British advance into Afghanistan to meet Russia, they ensure Afghan enmity against themselves and cause the Afghans to favour Russian interests. If Russia should send missions to, or set up agencies in, Afghanistan adverse to British interests, he would waste no remonstrances on the Afghans, believing them to be unwilling recipients of Russian messages, and to be more sinned against than sinning. He would remonstrate direct with Russia herself, and would let her see diplomatically that behind these remonstrances were ironclads and battalions. He was for telling her in time of peace, courteously but firmly, that she would not be allowed to interfere in Afghanistan or in any country contiguous to India. But if a general war were to break out, and if Russia not having been stopped by British counter-operations in Europe, were to advance towards India, then on no account would he meet her in Afghanistan. That, he affirmed, would be wasting our resources in men and money, and would be playing into the enemy's hands. The Afghans would, he supposed, be bitterly hostile to such advance, even though cowed into momentary submission. In that case he would help them with money and material, though not with men. Thus strengthened they might hamper the movements or retard the advance of the Russians; but be that as it might, he would have the British stand made on the British frontier. If the God of battles should then steel the hearts of British soldiers as of yore, the Russian invasion would, he trusted, be repelled decisively; and then the Russian retreat through Afghanistan, with the dreadful guerilla warfare of the Afghans, would be a spectacle to serve as a warning to invaders for all time coming.

Such is the substance of the opinion which he held rightly or wrongly, and for the vindication of which he exhausted every form of expression in private letters, in official despatches, and in conversations innumerable. His policy was once described by a friendly writer in the *Edinburgh Review* as "masterly inactivity," which expression contained both truth and error, and was regretted as being liable to misconstruction by the British public.

His views respecting the Russo-Afghan question were finally stated during the first days of January, 1869, in one of the last official letters of importance that he, with his Council, ever addressed to the Secretary of State in London.

"Should a foreign Power, such as Russia, ever seriously think of invading India from without, or, what is more probable, of stirring up the elements of disaffection or anarchy within it, our true policy, our strongest security, would then, we conceive, be found to lie in previous absence from entanglements at either Cabul, Candahar, or any similar outpost; in full reliance on a compact, highly equipped, and disciplined army stationed within our own territories, or on our own border; in the contentment, if not in the attachment, of the masses; in the sense of security of title and possession, with which our whole policy is gradually imbuing the minds of the principal chiefs and the native aristocracy; in the construction of material works within British India, which enhance the comfort of the people while they add to our political and military strength; in husbanding our finances and consolidating and multiplying our resources; in quiet preparation for all contingencies which no honest Indian statesman should disregard."

He repeated the same conclusion in his reply to the company at a farewell banquet on the evening of his last day in office, a speech which was his final utterance in India. Repelling the oft-repeated charge of inactivity in Central Asia, and speaking in the presence of many who knew all the details, he declared that he had watched most carefully all that went on in those distant regions; that he had abstained from interference there because such a course would lead to wars of which no man could foresee the end, would involve India in vast expenses which must lead to such an increase of taxation as would render British rule unpopular. Our true policy, he declared, is to avoid such complications, to consolidate our power in India, to give its people the best government we can, to organise our administration in every department by a combination of efficiency with economy. This he seemed to regard as his political testament on leaving India.

To show how these principles remained fast in his mind to the very end of life, two passages may be quoted from public letters which he dictated within the last twelvemonth before his death, after he had been literally half blinded by illness, when he was bowed down with infirmity and no longer able to read or write; and yet they remind the reader of his best manner.

Regarding the people of Afghanistan, he says:

"The Afghan is courageous, hardy, and independent; the country he lives in is strong and sterile in a remarkable degree, extraordinarily adapted for guerilla warfare; these people will never cease to resist so long as they have a hope of success, and, when beaten down, they have that kind of elasticity which will ever lead them to renew the struggle whenever opportunity of so doing may occur. If we enter Afghanistan, whether it be to punish the people for the alleged faults of their chiefs or to rectify our frontier, they will assuredly do all in their power to resist us. We want them as friends and not as enemies. In the latter category, they are extremely dangerous to us."

In respect of our policy towards them he repeats:

"So far as diplomacy and diplomacy alone, is concerned, we should do all in our power to induce the Afghans to side with us. We ought not, in my mind, to make an offensive and defensive treaty with them. This has been for many years their desire; but the argument against it is that if we made such a treaty, we should be bound to restrain them from any attacks on their neighbours, and to resent such assaults on them, while it would be next to impossible for us to ascertain the merits of such complaints. We should thus constantly find ourselves in a position to please neither party, and even bound to defend causes in which the Afghans were to blame."

Towards the end of 1868, having obtained the approval of the Government in England, he arranged a personal conference with the Amir Shir Ali, to be held at some place in British territory for settling the terms on which a limited support by subsidies in arms and money might be accorded to a friendly and independent Afghanistan. But he waited in vain for Shir Ali, who, though anxious to come, was prevented from doing so by some passing troubles near at home. This was in December, 1868, and his stay in India was fast drawing to a close, as his successor, Lord Mayo, was expected to arrive at Calcutta the following month, January, 1869. So the plan, to which he had obtained the sanction of the British Government, was unavoidably left to be carried out by his successor after a personal meeting with Shir Ali at some early date; and this actually took place at Umballa in the ensuing spring.

The night before the arrival of his successor, he attended the farewell banquet given in his honour by some two hundred and fifty gentlemen representing the European community of Calcutta. His public services were reviewed by the chairman, Sir William Mansfield (afterwards Lord Sandhurst), the Commander-in-Chief. His services respecting military supplies and transport in 1846, and regarding reinforcements for the army in 1857, were specially attested by Mansfield, a most competent judge speaking from personal knowledge; and then his subsequent career was reviewed in statesman-like and eloquent terms. When he rose to reply his voice was not resonant and his manner seemed hesitating, but the hesitation arose from the varied emotions that were surging in his breast, and the counter trains of thought that were coursing through his mind, as "the hours to their last minute were mounting" for his Indian career. Doffing his armour after a long course of victory, and arriving at that final end which entitles the victor to be called fortunate, he might well have been cheerful; but, on the contrary, he was somewhat melancholy—and his bearing then, compared to what it was when he landed in Calcutta, shewed how heavily the last five years had told upon him. His speech was characteristic as might have been expected. He reviewed his own policy in a concise and comprehensive manner; he said a good word for the inhabitants of North-western India, among whom his laborious lot had long been cast, attributing much of his success to the officers, his own countrymen, who had worked with him; and, as a peroration, he commended the Natives of India to the kindly sympathies of all whom his words might reach.

The next day he wore full dress for the reception of his successor, Lord Mayo, according to usage. The gilded uniform and the glittering decorations compared strangely with his wan look and toilworn frame. His veteran aspect presented a complete contrast to that of his handsome and gallant successor. He looked like a man whose conduct was as crystal and whose resolution as granite. He was indeed prematurely aged, for being only fifty-eight years old, he would, according to a British standard, be within the cycle of activity. His faithful friends, and they were legion, saw in him the representative of Anglo-Indian greatness. The same could not be said of his predecessors: the greatness of Wellesley, of Dalhousie, of Canning was not wholly of this character, but his greatness was Anglo-Indian solely and absolutely. Like

Warren Hastings, the first in the illustrious line of Governors-General, he had been appointed entirely for merit and service, without reference to parliamentary considerations or political influences; and again, like Warren Hastings, he had been instrumental in saving the empire from the stress of peril.

CHAPTER X

CONCLUSION

1869-1879

On March 15th, 1869, Sir John Lawrence landed in England after an absence of more than five years, his wife having preceded him thither the year before. The friends, who welcomed his return, thought him looking worn and broken. He was immediately raised to the peerage under the title of Baron Lawrence of the Punjab and Grateley. The Prime Minister (Mr. Gladstone), in the kindest terms, communicated to him the pleasure of the Sovereign. For his armorial bearings he characteristically adopted as supporters, two native Indian soldiers, a Sikh and a Mahommedan, in order to perpetuate, so far as might be possible, the remembrance of what he and his country owed to the men of these classes. The name Grateley he took from the small estate on Salisbury Plain which his sister Letitia, Mrs. Hayes, had left him on her death. His home at Southgate had been transferred to Queen's Gate in South Kensington; and he very soon made a short tour to Lynton to see his sister's grave, and to Clifton near Bristol, the home of his childhood.

In the spring of 1869, then, Lord Lawrence took his seat on the cross benches of the House of Lords, apparently indicating that he had not as yet attached himself formally to either political party, though he certainly continued to be, what he had always been, a very moderate Liberal in politics, anxious to preserve all the good institutions which the nation possesses, while striving for such reforms as might prove to be just, expedient or needful. His first rising in his place to say a few words, on a matter relating to the organisation of the Council of India at Whitehall, was greeted with significant cheers from both sides of the House of Lords. At that time the Bill for disestablishing the Irish Church was before Parliament, and in his heart he grieved over this measure, being much moved by all the Ulster associations of his youth, and well acquainted with all the considerations from a Churchman's point of view through his wife's relations or connexions. His regret was even intensified by his respect and esteem for the Ministry of that day, especially for the Duke of Argyll, and for the political party which comprised many of his best friends. When the Bill came to the Lords from the Commons, he followed with keen but melancholy interest the important debates which ensued, without however taking any part in them. He voted for the second reading, in the belief that resistance to the main principle of the measure had become hopeless in the circumstances, and that it only remained for the friends of the Church in the House of Lords to try and make the terms of disestablishment more favourable to her than those offered by the House of Commons, and to preserve as much of her property as possible. He rejoiced when the

House of Lords succeeded in doing much towards this end.

At this time the loss of the troopship *Megæra*, off the south-western coast of Africa, attracted much public attention ; the Government appointed a Commission of Inquiry of which he accepted the chairmanship. Much evidence was taken and an elaborate report made, into all which business he threw his wonted energy.

During the summer of 1869 his aspect brightened in the English air, and the tired look began to disappear, as if the oppression of care had been lightened. His circumstances were easy, and his means were adequate for his requirements with that good management which he always gave to his affairs. Though the inevitable gaps had been made by death among his relations and connexions, still his domestic circle was more than ordinarily peaceful and fortunate. His daughters were being married happily, and his sons were growing up or entering the world successfully. Thus the first year of his final return home drew to its close favourably. The next year, 1870, he spent placidly at Queen's Gate, Kensington, recruiting his strength, until the autumn, which for him became eventful.

He found that the Elementary Education Act had come into effect, and that a great School Board for all London was to be assembled, representing the several divisions of the metropolis. The elections took place in November, and having accepted a nomination by the ratepayers of his district, Chelsea, he was elected to be one of the members. When the members of the Board assembled in the Guildhall, he was chosen by them to be their Chairman, with Mr. C. Reed (afterwards Sir Charles) as Vice-Chairman. His acceptance of this position, within a short time after relinquishing the Government of India and returning to England, gladdened his friends as proving at least a partial recovery of health, but also surprised them. Thankless drudgery, as they thought, would be his lot, while wearisome debates would tax his patience, and a multiplicity of details would harass one who had been bred amidst stirring affairs in distant lands. Some even wondered whether such work as this would be for him *dignus vindice nodus.* He thought otherwise however; and his immediate recognition, at the very outset, of the great future in store for the London School Board, is a token of his prescience and sagacity. He shared the anxiety then felt by many lest the education given in the Board Schools should fail to include religious instruction, and he decided for this reason among others to put his massive shoulder to the wheel. He had the happiness soon to see this instruction properly afforded. The work, too, was for the children of the labouring poor, and —while looking towards high education with due deference—he had fixed his heart always on elementary education. In India he rejoiced in village schools, and during his sojourn in England he had given attention to the schools near his house at Southgate. Having accepted the Chairmanship, he was prepared not only to guide the deliberations of the Board in a statesmanlike manner, but also to take a personally active part in its business. The permanent officers of the Board still remember the ardour and enthusiasm which he seemed to throw into the work. Much as it might differ from that to which he had long been used, yet he remembered the command,—that which thy hand findeth to do, do it with all thy might.

On this Board he found many members in company with whom any man might be glad to act: Lord Sandon (now Earl of Harrowby), Lord Mahon (the present Earl Stanhope), Mr. W. H. Smith (now leader of the House of Commons), Professor Huxley, Samuel Morley, the Reverend Anthony Thorold (now Bishop of Rochester), and others. He presided regularly at the weekly meetings, and when the executive business came to be done by several committees, he attended them also with the utmost assiduity. On this occasion, as on other occasions in his life, the acceptance of fresh work seemed to have an electric effect on him. After the lapse of seventeen years the operations of the Board are seen by all men to be vast, probably the largest of their kind under any one Board in the world; but in his day there was at first only a small beginning. The number of children in the metropolis at voluntary schools (elementary) of all kinds was little over three hundred thousand, too few for a population of more than four millions, so the Board under his presidency was to ascertain the total number of children of a school-going age, then about three-quarters of a million, deduct therefrom the number actually at voluntary schools, and for the remainder (technically called the deficiency) provide Board Schools, after making allowance for those who must unavoidably be absent.

In the very first instance he and his colleagues had to arrange the working of the Board itself, which, as a representative body of considerable importance, needed rules to be framed for the conduct of its debates. He soon found the benefit of a definite procedure, because public elementary education was new, and many questions which having been since settled are now regarded as beyond dispute, were then in an inchoate condition, and tossed about with diverse forces of argument. Many of his colleagues were positive thinkers, fluent debaters, and persons with independent or original ideas, so he had to preside patiently over protracted discussions on grave subjects wherein, after a survey of the arguments, his own mind was soon made up. So fast has been the progress of public opinion, that nowadays, after the lapse of seventeen years, we may wonder at the heat and pertinacity with which several educational topics were debated before him: such as the exercise of the powers for compelling attendance at the schools,—the introduction of sound religious teaching,—the principles on which the Board should calculate the educational wants which it was to supply,—the curriculum of the subjects which should be taught in the schools, as coming within the scope of elementary education,—the part to be taken by the Board in carrying into effect the beneficent principles of the Industrial Schools Act throughout the metropolitan area,—the gradation of the fees payable by the scholars, and so on. He rejoiced in the Resolution passed by the Board in 1871, that "The Bible should be read, and that there should be given such explanations and such instructions therefrom in the principles of religion and morality as are suited to the capacity of children; provided that no attempt be made to attach children to any particular denomination."

He and his colleagues saw at once that the administration of so growing a business as this could not be conducted by a deliberative body of more than fifty members assembled once a week. He and they knew that the executive work must really be done in Committees. So he arranged that on one or more of the Committees every member of the Board should serve, and that the recommendations of each Committee should be brought up to the weekly meetings of the whole Board, for adoption, or for such other orders as might be passed. Thus he saw those several Committees constituted,—which have during the subsequent sixteen years done what must be termed a mighty work,—for determining the provision of school-places, according to the needs of the population,—for procuring, and if necessary enforcing by law, the attendance at school,—for distributing the large staff of teachers among a great number of schools,—for dealing with the waif and stray children in the streets,—for the purchase of sites for school-houses in densely peopled quarters, and for the erection of buildings,—for managing the debt which the Board must incur in building school-houses,—and for determining annually the amount to be levied by precept from the rate-payers of the metropolis.

He also saw a Divisional Committee appointed for each of the ten electoral divisions of the metropolis, to consist of the members of the Board representing that division with the assistance of local residents. Then his Board furnished the Divisional Committees with a staff of Visitors whose duty it was to make a house-to-house visitation, and to register every child of a school-going age throughout the metropolis, so that the attendance of all might be by degrees enforced; and this far-reaching organisation still exists.

The elections being triennial, his Board, which had been elected as the first Board in November, 1870, yielded place to its successor in November, 1873. He then, from fatigue which necessitated repose, resigned the Chairmanship after three years' incumbency, and did not seek re-election as a member. In fact, within his term, he had been once obliged to be absent for a few months on account of sleeplessness attributable to mental exertion. At the last meeting of his Board a vote of thanks was accorded to him, on the motion of Samuel Morley seconded by W. H. Smith, for the invariable kindness and ability which he had evinced in the Chair.

Then it was announced that £400 had been contributed by members of the Board in order to form a scholarship to perpetuate the memory of his chairmanship, and £1000 were added by the Duke of Bedford "in order to mark his sense of the services of Lord Lawrence and of the Board over which his Lordship had presided." The permanent officers of the Board caused a portrait of him to be painted, which now hangs in the large hall of the Board-meetings right over the Chair which is occupied by his successors. A banquet was given in his honour by his colleagues, at which a tribute to his labours in the Board was paid by Mr. W. E. Forster, then a member of the Government, as vice-president of the Council.

It may be well to cite some brief passages to show the estimation in which he was held by the Board.

When the vote of thanks on his retirement was proposed, Mr. Samuel Morley, speaking as "an acknowledged Non-conformist," said that gentlemen of the most opposite opinions had been able to work together harmoniously, and this result he attributed in a large measure to the character of the Chairman. Mr. W. H. Smith said "the way in which Lord Lawrence came forward had greatly tended to rouse the minds of the people to the absolute duty of providing for the education of the destitute children, not only of London, but of England." Another member said "his friends out of doors, the working classes, would find fault with him if he did not on their behalf tender their thanks to Lord Lawrence."

From his reply one significant sentence may be quoted as showing that his Board had been friendly to the Voluntary system of education in the metropolis. "We have in no way trodden upon those who have gone before us, or done anything to injure them, but on the contrary our sympathies and feelings have been in the main with those who have preceded us, and all we desired to do was to supplement the good work which they had begun."

Lastly, at the banquet Mr. Forster said that "the greatest compliment he could pay to the Board would be to say that the work of the last three years will not be the least interesting part of the history of Lord Lawrence, and will bear comparison with many another passage in that history."

Thus ended the crowning episode in the story of his public life. He who had been the master of many legions, had used the pomp and circumstance of the East for exerting beneficent influence, had defended an empire during war and guided it in progressive ways during peace—now rejoiced that the sunset of his career should be gilded by services to the poor of London.

He continued, however, to take interest in matters cognate to education. Being one of the Vice-Presidents of the Church Missionary Society, he frequently attended the meetings of its General Committee. Once at a gathering held in furtherance of the mission cause, he bore testimony on behalf of the Missionaries in India, with words that are affectionately cherished by all whom they concern.

"I believe that, notwithstanding all that the people of England have done to benefit India (that is, by philanthropic effort), the Missionaries have done more than all other agencies combined. They have had arduous and uphill work, often receiving no encouragement, and have had to bear the taunts and obloquy of those who despised and disliked their preaching. But such has been the effect of their earnest zeal, untiring devotion, and of the excellent example which they have universally shown, that in spite of the great masses of the people being opposed to their doctrine, they are, as a body, popular in the country. I have a great reverence and regard for them, both personally and for the sake of the great cause in which they are engaged."

In his three months' absence, already mentioned, during his incumbency in the School Board for London, he visited at Paris the scenes of the Franco-German war and subsequent disturbances there. He also renewed his recollections of Rome and Naples. Since 1871 he had taken for a summer residence the beautiful Brockett Hall in Hertfordshire, fragrant with the memories of Palmerston, and he kept it till the autumn of 1875. The place and its surroundings always delighted him. The last years of physical comfort that he was destined to enjoy were spent there. He appeared to think himself old, though he was hardly so in years, being then sixty-five; but over-exertion during his life of action may have aged him prematurely. To his friends he would write that old age was creeping over him.

Early in 1876 the eyes, which had been keen-sighted originally but had for many years troubled him occasionally, began to fail, and an operation was afterwards performed in London. During the summer he suffered dreadful pain, and had for weeks to be kept in complete darkness. From this misery he emerged in the autumn with one eye sightless and the other distressfully weak. In the spring of the following year, 1877, he submitted to a further operation, and took up his abode in London at Queen's Gate Gardens. Though unable to read or write, he was relieved from the fear of blindness; so he made a short tour in the New Forest, and attended the House of Lords occasionally during the summer. In the autumn he visited Inverness, and was thankful on finding himself able to read the Bible in large print. For the winter he returned to Queen's Gate Gardens, and in August of the next year, 1878, he moved for a while to Broadstairs in the Isle of Thanet. Soon he began to take an anxious interest in the intelligence from Afghanistan, which was then agitating the public mind in Britain. He dictated several letters to the *Times*, reiterating with the old force and clearness his well-known views on Afghan policy, which have been set forth in the preceding chapter. He in conjunction with some of his political friends pressed the Government in London for the production of papers that might elucidate the circumstances, which had led to the military operations by the British against Afghanistan, and especially the conduct, as proved or surmised, of the Amir Shir Ali. He saw, however, that events came thick and fast; the war advanced apace, and was followed by a treaty with Shir Ali's son Yakoob ; the papers were produced in England, and the whole matter was disposed of in Parliament by a late autumn session.

Early in 1879 he seemed fairly well, though he himself had felt warnings of the coming end. But in the spring he paid flying visits to Edinburgh and Manchester. In May he made a wedding-speech on the marriage of his second son. On June 19th he attended the House of Lords for the last time. His object in so doing was to make a speech on a License Tax which had recently been imposed in India. He did not object to such taxes being introduced there to touch the rich and the comparatively prosperous middle classes; indeed he had levied such himself. But he deprecated them extremely if they reached the poor, and he was apprehensive lest this particular tax should go too far in that direction. Therefore he wished to raise his voice on the subject. But it was with him that day as it had been with dying statesmen before, and the sad history repeated itself. His once resonant voice, his strong nerve, his retentive memory, failed him in some degree, and he was not able to deliver fully a speech for which he had made preparations with his wonted carefulness. Yet it was fitting, even poetically meet, that this supreme effort of his should have been put forth on behalf of the industrial poor for whom he had ever cared at home and abroad. However he sat out the debate and drove home exhausted. During the ensuing days drowsiness set in, and he, the indefatigable worker at last complained of fatigue. But for the briefest while he revived enough to attend to private business. He was present, too, at an anniversary meeting on behalf of the asylum at Hampstead for the orphan daughters of soldiers, and proposed a vote of thanks to the Duchess of Connaught. The next day the sleepiness again overtook him, and continued for the two following days, though he aroused himself enough to attend to business. Then he became too weak to leave his bed, and shortly afterwards died peacefully, surrounded by those who were nearest and dearest to him.

Two statues are standing in memory of him; one opposite the Government House at Calcutta, on the edge of that famous plain, called the Mydan, which is being gradually surrounded with monuments of British heroism and genius; the other at Waterloo Place in London, side by side with Clyde and face to face with Franklin. No stately inscriptions commemorate his achievements in classic terms. His friends deemed it best to engrave his great name on the stone, with the simplest particulars of time and place.

But the most sympathetically human demonstration was that at the funeral on July 5th, when his body was laid "to mingle with the illustrious dust" in Westminster Abbey. The Queen and the Prince of Wales were each represented in this closing scene. All the renowned Anglo-Indians then in England were present. The gathering, too, comprised much that was representative of Britain in war and peace, in art, literature and statesmanship. The decorations of the officers, won in Eastern service, shone amidst the dark colours of mourning. The words of the anthem were "his body is buried in peace but his name liveth for evermore." As the coffin was lowered, the concluding lines of the hymn were sung:

> "And at our Father's loved abode
> Our souls arrive in peace."

The funeral sermon was preached in the choir by Dean Stanley, who exclaimed as he ended: "Farewell, great Proconsul of our English Christian empire! Where shall we look in the times that are coming for that disinterested love, that abounding knowledge of India, like his? Where shall we find that resolution of mind and countenance which seemed to say to us,

> 'This rock shall fly
> From its firm base as soon as I'?"

THE END